LOOKING AFTER
YOUR MAC
MADE EASY

This is a **FLAME TREE** book
First published 2014

Publisher and Creative Director: Nick Wells
Project Editor: Polly Prior
Art Director and Layout Design: Mike Spender
Digital Design and Production: Chris Herbert
Copy Editor: Anna Groves
Technical Reader: Mark Mayne
Proofreader: Amanda Crook
Screenshots: Chris Smith

Special thanks: Laura Bulbeck, Emma Chafer, Esme Chapman, Helen Snaith

This edition first published 2014 by
FLAME TREE PUBLISHING
Crabtree Hall, Crabtree Lane
Fulham, London SW6 6TY
United Kingdom

www.flametreepublishing.com

14 16 18 17 15
1 3 5 7 9 10 8 6 4 2

© 2014 Flame Tree Publishing

ISBN 978-1-78361-136-2

A CIP record for this book is available from the British Library upon request.

Printed in China

All Apple product shots are © 2014 Apple Inc.; all other non-screenshot pictures are courtesy of Shutterstock: 25, 32, 34, 38, 157, 174,
193, 219, 221, 230, 245 and © the following photographers: aastock: 7, 212; Andrey Bayda: 4, 14; kazoka: 2; Dragon Images : 5, 84;
Goodluz: 132, 191; Chayatorn Laorattanavech: 97; Dmitry Lobanov: 76; Eugenio Marongiu: 162; imagedb.com: 204; Kirill__M : 6, 152;
ra2studio: 6, 136; sdecoret: 5, 42; sheff: 7, 182; Tomislav Stajduhar: 227; tkemot: 222

LOOKING AFTER
YOUR MAC
MADE EASY

CHRIS SMITH

FLAME TREE
PUBLISHING

CONTENTS

If you're yet to plump for a brand new Mac and you're still weighing up your options, this chapter will furnish you with all the information you need to make sure you come home with the perfect model for your needs. You'll also learn about the advantages of using a Mac over a PC and the best accessories to augment your Mac. Finally, we'll get that new Mac out of the box and introduce and explain some of its physical features, before getting it ready for action.

GETTING STARTED

This chapter will guide you through the initial set-up process and explain the basics of the Mac OS X operating system. You'll learn your way around the user interface, how to master the dock, take a trip around the software with Finder, get connected to the Internet, learn the basics of using applications, and master some neat multi-touch gestures for good measure.

PUTTING YOUR MAC TO WORK

Now all of the basics are out of the way, we'll really start to pick up the pace in this chapter. We'll learn the intricacies of the Safari web browser, get productive, get organized, and set up your email, messaging and social-networking accounts. We'll also give you the low-down on finding and downloading apps, and organizing your photo collection and storing it safely on your Mac.

A shorter chapter aimed at helping you get the most out of your digital movie and music collection through iTunes. We'll also introduce the iBooks store and the possibilities for gaming on your Mac.

Now we're getting into the technical stuff. Within these pages, you'll learn how to create the perfect home network, incorporating all of your accessories and home entertainment equipment. We'll also explore other ways to get connected, how to create computer-to-computer networks, and how to share files with other devices.

PROTECTING YOUR MAC

Here you'll learn to safeguard your precious documents, photographs, media files and applications. You'll learn how to back up your Mac, master the powerful iCloud and Time Machine tools, and we'll also give you all of the information you need to keep your Mac secure from unwanted intrusion.

TROUBLESHOOTING

Are you struggling with a maddeningly slow Mac? Unable to access your files? Enduring terrible battery life? Fret not, we've got the solution. And, if your Mac encounters a serious problem beyond our expertise, we'll point you in the right direction.

INTRODUCTION

If you're reading this book, then congratulations are in order. You've either decided to buy a Mac computer, or you've already taken the leap into a brave new world of computing. Whether this is your first computer, or you're taking a journey into the unknown from the familiarity of a Windows PC, you've come to the right place. By the time you're through with this book, you'll be a Mac master, an expert at setting up and getting the most out of the software, able to protect your important data and squash any problems you may encounter. We're excited and we hope you are too.

Yum.

Think different.

WHAT CAN I DO WITH A MAC?

One of the questions we get asked most often is: 'Can a Mac do everything a PC can?' The answer is a resounding yes, and then some. As you'll discover, it's a productivity-enhancing device for work and school, a comprehensive communications tool for messaging, video chatting and emailing, and it's perfect for getting the most out of the Internet and social networks. It's a multimedia powerhouse, a navigation tool, a personal organizer, and a place to store and share your photos. If you're a creative type, then there are tons of powerful apps you can use to make your vision a reality. What more could you ask?

Left: Macs have the capabilities to do everything PCs can, and may even be more suited to certain purposes, particularly creative projects.

Above: The design of Mac computers is constantly changing and improving, with the latest versions looking particularly sleek and slim.

A QUICK HISTORY LESSON

Mac is short for Macintosh, the line of computers created by American technology giant, Apple. You know, the guys who have since become more famous for the iPod, iTunes, iPad and iPhone. Apple's history runs deep. It was co-founded by the late Steve Jobs in 1976 and, before the Microsoft monopoly took over, a Macintosh was the first computer in many homes during the revolution of the 1980s. Apple faded as Windows dominated the 1990s, but thanks to stunning design and intuitive software, Apple has bounced back strongly in the 21st century. What's more, if you're one of the millions who owns an iPhone or an iPad, you're going to get even more out of your Mac!

WHICH MAC IS BEST FOR ME?

Macs might be in the minority when it comes to the number of Windows PCs on sale, but that doesn't mean there isn't a host of awesome options to choose from. If you've already chosen your Mac, you're all set, but if you're still deliberating, the first part of Chapter One will help you work out which Apple computer is best for you. From the ultra-portable MacBook Air, to a 27-inch desktop iMac. We'll also help you calculate how much processing power, memory and storage you'll need.

THE MAC OS X SOFTWARE

All Apple Mac computers run off built-in software that's made by Apple and Apple only. It's called Mac OS X, meaning the tenth version of the Macintosh Operating System. The current version is Mac OS X 10.9 (aka Mavericks). If you're on a Mac bought in the last few years, you can upgrade to Mavericks for free. If you're buying a new Mac, it's built right in when you switch on for the first time. We think you'll find it intuitive and easy to use. We'll be talking through the features assuming you're using Mac OS X 10.9 Mavericks. Where features are new in Mavericks we'll make you aware, in case you're on an older version.

Above: Throughout this book we will discuss how to use Mac OS X software, both current and older versions where there are differences.

USING THIS BOOK

While this book has been written with a logical chronology – from buying a Mac, to setting it up, to learning the software and putting it to work – it doesn't mean you need to read it from cover to cover. We hope that you'll dive in whenever you need help or something explained in simple terms. We've also given special consideration to Chapters Six and Seven. They'll help you look after your new computer as well as navigate the myriad issues and problems that can pop up with any complex electronic device.

Easily Digestible

Make no mistake, there's a LOT of information contained within the next 250 or so pages, but there's no need to be intimidated. As far as possible, we've broken it down into bite-sized chunks. In some areas we'll offer a general explanation of features and their capabilities, while

Hot Tips!

Throughout the book, we've inserted a host of bonus tips from our years of experience using Macs. These suggestions or shortcuts may be less obvious or even hidden away, but can be the key to unlocking extra features and getting more out of your Mac.

in others there'll be detailed step-by-step instructions. We've also illustrated many of the features with screenshots so you can see what you're doing. In order to get the most out of this book, we suggest you're seated in front of your Mac as you read.

Jargon Busting

It's true that some jargon is unavoidable, but wherever possible we've attempted to explain and break down technical terms in easy-to-understand language.

Seven Chapters

While we've chosen to spread the path to becoming a Mac expert across seven clearly defined chapters, we'll nudge you in and out of other chapters when features overlap. Chapter One is all about finding the perfect Mac for you and getting it set up. Chapter Two guides you through the initial set-up and will familiarize you with the basic features of the Mac OS X operating system. In Chapter Three you'll put your Mac to work, and in Chapter Four we'll have a little fun with music and video content. In Chapter Five we'll perfect networking in home and public, while Chapter Six is all about protecting your Mac and the information stored within. In Chapter Seven we'll run through a host of common problems and zap them one by one, and if we can't zap them, we'll point you in the direction of someone who can!

Left: You will be guided through all the basics to get you started, such as setting up an internet connection.

Above: Chapter Four will discuss everything you need to know about working with music and videos on your Mac.

Apptastic

If you've just spent around £1,000 ($1,600) on a new Mac, the last thing you want to do is spend a fortune on expensive programmes. With that in mind, we've focused on the apps that are built in with your Mac, mentioning other freebies here and there. However, at the end of the book you'll find a list of 100 fantastic apps you can download to take your user experience to the next level.

About The Author

Chris Smith is a freelance technology journalist for some of the UK's most respected websites and publications. Chris has been using, testing and reviewing Macs for over ten years and has written countless articles about Apple computers, software and applications during that time.

SETTING UP

WHAT IS A MAC COMPUTER?

Mac computers are made by Apple and Apple only. That's the same company that's responsible for the wildly successful and popular iPhone smartphones, iPad tablets and iPod music players. Before the mobile gadgets took over, Macs were where it all started for Apple. The company launched its first home computer in 1984 and after disappearing into the wilderness during the 1990s, it's remerged with a vengeance over the last decade.

WHAT MAKES A MAC DIFFERENT?

Other than the hardware designed and built by Apple, what distinguishes Mac computers from the personal computers you may be used to? Mainly, it's the software. Computers with the Apple logo operate on the Mac OS X (Macintosh Operating System 10) rather than the Microsoft-build Windows software that most PC users will be used to. Mac OS X software behaves very differently to the Windows operating system, but different can be good and is assuredly so in this instance.

Left: The first Apple Macintosh home computer.

WHICH MAC IS BEST FOR YOU?

There are lots of different Mac models around so it's very important to choose the correct computer to suit your needs. Do you work a lot on the go, or do you need a powerful machine, with a big display for your home office? Here are your options.

Apple iMac

The iMac is Apple's staple desktop computer, and is great for the home office. The newest models are things of real beauty.
The iMac comes in an all-in-one package with all of the computing technology housed within a thin, fully adjustable display. The iMac comes in 21-inch or 27-inch models.

MacBook Pro

The MacBook Pro brings all of the power and functionality of a desktop iMac in one portable, lightweight package that can be carried around with you wherever you go. Naturally, this laptop computer comes with the display, keyboard and trackpad integrated within in one neat package and has a 13-inch screen.

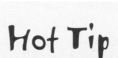

Hot Tip
The Mac Pro is only really for those needing to deal with massive amounts of data at high speed, well beyond what would be required by the vast majority of computer users.

Above: The MacBook Pro with Retina Display, with its high resolution screen, is perfect for video or photo editing.

MacBook Pro With Retina Display

A couple of years ago Apple launched a new version of the MacBook Pro, with a super high-resolution screen it likes to call the 'Retina Display'. The resolution is 2560 x 1600, which means it has greater pixel density than your HD television at home. The luxury 13-inch and 15-inch MacBook Pro with Retina Display is more expensive than the standard model, but it's great for those who need a crystal-clear display for things like photo and video editing.

MacBook Air

The ultra-portable MacBook Air laptop might just be the star of the whole show. It weighs as little as 2.38 lbs, is 0.11 inches at its thinnest point and is just 0.68 inches at its thickest point. It comes in 11.6-inch and 13.3-inch flavours and promises up to 12-hours of battery life. It still packs plenty of power and is perfect for those who are always on the go or who don't want a heavier device sitting on their laps all day. They're also the cheapest of the range.

Mac Pro

The new Mac Pro is the most powerful and unique-looking computer Apple has ever produced. The black cylinder is less than 10 inches tall and can furnish up to a 12-core processor. It starts at a whopping £2,499/$2,999.

Mac Mini

The Mac Mini is a good option for those who already have a monitor, mouse and keyboard. The Mac Mini box, named for its diminutive size, simply connects to your existing accessories.

Ideal Use Cases

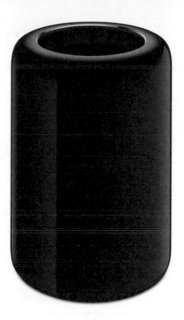

Above: The Mac Pro looks like a small black cylinder and is extremely powerful.

- ◯ **MacBook Air**: Light user, Internet surfer, email addict, traveller, writer, commuter.

- ◯ **MacBook Pro**: On-the-go power user, working from home, designer, music editor.

- ◯ **MacBook Pro with Retina Display**: The above + photo/video editor, designer, movie fan.

- ◯ **iMac 27-inch**: Slave to the desk, movie fan and design fetishist.

- ◯ **Mac Pro**: Professional HD video editor, web designer music producer, game developer.

WHERE ARE ALL THE TOUCH SCREEN MACS?

Short answer? There aren't any and there aren't likely to be any anytime soon. Apple has been reluctant to cannibalize Macs and iPads by creating a hybrid model because the company believes there is room in our living rooms (if not our bank balance) for both. If you want a touch screen Mac, the closest you'll get is an Apple iPad and a Bluetooth wireless keyboard. Failing that, it'll be one of the many Windows 8.1 tablet/laptop hybrids. But before you do that, read on.

MAC VERSUS WINDOWS

The on-going war between Mac and personal computers running Microsoft's Windows operating system continues to rage. Quite frankly, and depending on your sport, it's the technological equivalent of Liverpool and Manchester United, Borg and McEnroe or Muhammad Ali and Joe Frazier.

THE RIVALRY: A POTTED HISTORY

The first versions of the Apple Mac dominated the 1980s and for many households it was their first computer. Apple somewhat lost its way in the 1990s and, largely as a result of the launch of Windows 3.0 in 1990, Microsoft assumed the dominant position it still holds today. By that time home computers were almost as prevalent as the television set. Apple fought back in the Noughties (or whatever we're calling them) with the launch of the Mac OS X software (a huge upgrade), but Mac ownership still makes up the minority.

Above: Mac launched the OS X software in the Noughties.

WHY CHOOSE A MAC?

As most people learn to use a computer using Windows, the change to Mac, which runs very different software and uses a slightly different keyboard, can be somewhat confusing. This book aims to assist you with the transition and to outline some of the benefits you can look forward to when you've made the switch.

No Viruses

Windows PCs are always going down with some kind of infection or ailment and require expensive anti-virus software to stave off terminal illness. Those threats are far less common on Mac computers, with very few recorded incidents of malicious software affecting users. Apple says 'no computer is 100 per cent safe', but its machines are *safer*.

Great Design

Generally speaking, Macs are infinitely better looking than their Windows-running counterparts. Design is Apple's thing. Heck, the company's British design guru Jonathan Ive was recently awarded a knighthood for it. Arise, Sir Jony!

Hot Tip

To learn about how to protect your Mac online, head on to Chapter Six (*see* pages 182–211).

Above: One of the most appealing things about Mac computers is the beauty of their design.

Space Saving And Portability

The all-in-one iMacs and the newest MacBook Air and MacBook Pro laptops defy modern physics with their ultra-thin and light designs. That's a big plus for modern users who don't want bulky tower PCs cluttering up the home, or to carry cumbersome laptops to work every day.

Intuitive Software

There's a saying among Apple fans: 'Once you go Mac, you never go back!' As soon as you've mastered the intricacies of the Mac OS X software, you'll wonder why you toiled for so long on Windows.

Powerful Tools For Creative Types

If you look at the creative industries – publishing, design, entertainment – all of the top dogs use Macs rather than PCs. If you're designing a magazine, editing video, producing music, Mac is where it's at. If your creative juices are overflowing, you're more likely to channel them using a Mac.

Above: Macs can often be a better choice for those working on creative projects.

Playing Nicely With iPhones And iPads

A lot of people become interested in owning a Mac because they love the user-friendly experience of using an iPad or iPhone. There's more symmetry than ever between Apple's mobile and computing software and, as you'd expect, these devices communicate very well with each other. Email, calendar documents, photos, music, video and more come together in one cosy ecosystem.

Speaking Of iPads …

Now because you've bought this book, or are at least reading it at your local library or bookstore, we're pretty sure you're set on buying a Mac. Not that we'd ever try to convince you otherwise, but before you do, answer these questions truthfully:

Above. iPads are compact and perfect for simple needs such as browsing the Internet and listening to music.

- Do you enjoy playing lots of games like **Angry Birds**?

- Do you plan to use your **Mac** mainly for looking at the Internet, emailing **friends**, watching **video** and listening to **music**?

- Do you prefer using **touch screen** devices to physical **keyboards**?

- Could you survive without access to full productivity programs like **word processors**, **photo editors** and **design tools**?

- Are you looking for the most **compact** package possible?

> ## Hot Tip
> Use iTunes and iPhoto on your Mac to back up and safeguard the data and photographs on your iPhone (*see* page 123).

If the answer to most or all of these questions is '**Yes**' then you may want to consider buying an iPad. Just sayin'.

WHAT TO LOOK FOR

Once you've decided which Mac model is for you, there are many configuration options to decide upon before completing your purchase. The most important of these are the display size, the amount of computing power (CPU), the memory (RAM) and the amount of built-in storage your device has. All of these can significantly affect the price, so choose wisely.

DISPLAY SIZE

This is kind of an obvious one and often the first and most important choice for users. MacBooks range from 11.6 inches to 15.4 inches. If portability is your key concern, then the 11.6-inch MacBook Air is for you. If you're editing photos or watching a lot of movies, then maybe choose the 15.4-inch MacBook Air. The same goes for the iMacs at 21 and 27 inches. Remember, the larger the screen, the larger the price.

PROCESSING POWER

When purchasing a Mac, either through the Apple Store or your local electronics retailer, they'll ask you about processors (CPU). The better the CPU, the more efficient your computer will be at performing the tasks asked of it. If you're only using your Mac for web browsing, document creation and emailing, you won't

Right: The processing power needed on your Mac computer will depend on the types of tasks likely to be performed.

need to overspend on CPU, but if you try power-hungry tasks on that machine, you'll see plenty of the annoying spinning beach ball (see page 217). Don't expect to edit high-definition video on a MacBook Air; for that you'll need a MacBook Pro or iMac.

- ○ **Intel Cores**: New Macs run on Intel Core i5 or i7 chips. The i7 chips represent higher performance and hence add to the cost of your Mac.

- ○ **Dual core or quad core**: A dual-core processor offers twice the speed of a single chip, while quad-core chips, which appear in iMacs, offer four times the power.

- ○ **Speed**: When choosing your processor you'll see a speed attached to the processor. That's how fast it's capable of running. A 2.7 GHz Intel Core i5 quad-core processor on an iMac will offer better performance than the 2.5 GHz Intel Core i5 processor.

MEMORY

A lot of people confuse memory with the amount of stuff you can store on your computer. That's not the case. RAM, which stands for Random Access Memory, is the computer's short-term memory, where all of your current tasks are handled. The more things you're doing on your Mac or the more power-hungry programs you're using, the more memory it takes up. The more memory your computer has to spare, the more efficiently it can accomplish these tasks. The MacBook Air's come with 4 GB RAM, right up to 64 GB on the Mac Pro. You can do the math there.

Hot Tip
On some MacBook models it's very difficult to add RAM due to the unibody casing. If you're in doubt, it's better to go big on memory when you buy your Mac.

STORAGE

This is where all of your files sit. If you have a massive personal music and video collection or a huge photo library to store on your Mac, then the 128 GB MacBook Air is going to fill up very quickly. Of course, more storage adds to the cost of your Mac.

Hot Tip

There are multiple ways to boost your storage. You can buy an external hard drive that plugs into your Mac, or use iCloud to store your files.

Above: One way to boost storage space is to connect an external hard drive to your Mac.

GRAPHICS

This isn't a huge concern for newcomers, but if you enjoy gaming on your device, then a better graphics card will be of assistance with the large transfers of visual data. Numerous configurations are available.

ACCESSORIZING

You've navigated the minefield of configuring your Mac, but before you hit the checkout button or hand over your credit card, you may want to accessorize your Mac. Here's some of the stuff you may need/want/can't afford but will buy anyway.

Optical Drive

The era of physical media seems to be coming to an end, in favour of an all-digital future. To that end, Apple has ditched disk drives (for DVDs and CDs) in all models but the basic 13-inch MacBook Pro.

Above: A Superdrive.

That means if you want to play your physical movie and music collection, you'll need a Superdrive. They cost £65/$79 and plug into your Mac's USB ports.

Mouse Or Trackpad?

When buying an iMac, you'll need to choose whether you want a traditional Apple mouse or a Magic Trackpad. Using the trackpad you'll navigate around the OS using your fingers on the flat surface and tapping to click. It's pretty cool once you're used to it, and when ordering from Apple it comes at no extra cost.

Above: A Magic Trackpad can be used to navigate the screen instead of a traditional mouse.

AirPort Time Capsule

We'll go into more detail about this in Chapters Five, Six and Seven, but the AirPort Time Capsule is an external hard drive that also backs up all of your data at regular intervals, wirelessly, saving your skin if something happens to your Mac. It's also a fully functioning wireless modem, too.

Printer

Thanks to the joys of email we don't kill nearly as many trees as we used to, but printers are still handy occasionally. Macs are compatible with wireless and wired USB printers, so take your pick. If you already have one at home, it should still hook up.

Right: The AirPort Time Capsule has multiple functions, including regularly backing up.

Who Needs A Scanner, Really?

When you buy your Mac, someone may try to sell you a scanner, but in all honesty, it's another computing peripheral that's outlived its usage thanks to digital media and email. These days, there's little need to scan in photos or documents for transmission. However, for those odd times, you may still want one.

External Hard Drive

If you choose an AirPort Time Capsule you're covered for storage space, otherwise you may want to buy an external hard drive in order to back up your documents and store media collections that have become too large for storage on your Mac. These supplemental storage drives plug in through the USB port or the Thunderbolt port on newer Macs.

Above: AirPlay can stream music and videos from iTunes.
Below: The Apple TV device sends content from the Mac to the TV.

External Speakers

All new Macs come with built-in speakers, but there's nothing wrong with boosting the sound output a little. Macs will hook up to any speakers with a 3.5-mm (headphone-sized) jack, but you may wish to look at AirPlay and Bluetooth speakers (see page 171) which allow you to beam audio from your Mac over the airwaves without being tethered to wires.

Apple TV

Imagine being able to send content from your computer directly to your HD television over the Internet! Well, it's pretty straightforward actually, thanks to the Apple TV device. As well as being able to send video to the big screen using AirPlay technology (see page 172), you can completely mirror what's on your Mac screen, making it great for showing photo slideshows or even presentations. The Apple TV costs £100/$100.

Need Wired Internet?

Mainly as a space-saving measure, which allows Macs to be more portable, Apple has foregone the Ethernet port on the MacBook Air, which means you can only connect to networks wirelessly. It's a bit of a pain sometimes, but if you still want or need to physically tether yourself to a network, you can buy a £25/$29 adapter with your Mac.

Protection

After splashing all this cash on a Mac, it'd be remiss not to give yourself a little protection. Here are a few ways to do this.

Above: AppleCare offers extended support after the initial 90 days warranty.

- **AppleCare**: When you buy a Mac you're covered by a one year limited warranty which covers you for repair or replacement when the issue is not your fault (drops, liquid damage, etc. aren't covered), but Apple's extended warranty programme covers you for damages after that period. You'll also get telephone support as well as free repairs for three years after the original purchase date.

- **Cases**: There is a huge array of cases, bags and clip-on shells to keep your MacBook in pristine condition and safeguard it against occasional drops and spills. Get one. You won't regret it.

Hot Tip

Brenthaven cases and backpacks come highly recommended, while the see-through, clip-on coatings from Speck are also very popular and will keep your Mac looking sharp. Shop around online for some good deals.

GETTING FAMILIAR WITH YOUR MAC

Okay, so you've finally chosen the Mac that best suits your needs and it's sitting there looking all pretty in a box in your living room. Before we jump into the joys of the Mac OS X software, let's take a tour around the hardware and get it set up properly.

UNBOXING YOUR MAC

Regardless of the time of year, there's something extremely Christmassy about unboxing a brand-new piece of tech, especially when it comes in as nice a box as an Apple iMac or MacBook! Let's take a look at what's inside.

What's In The Box?

The packaging is minimal because, unlike big PCs of yesteryear, there's not a lot in the box other than the essentials.

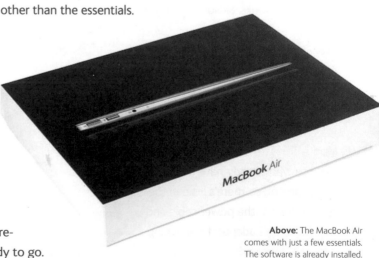

- ○ **MacBook Air/Pro:** When you open your MacBook, you'll find only the computer itself, the MagSafe power cable, an AC adapter and a little bit of documentation. All of the software is pre-installed, so you're ready to go.

Above: The MacBook Air comes with just a few essentials. The software is already installed.

Above: An iMac will come with a wireless keyboard, as well as a power cable and wireless mouse or trackpad.

- **iMac:** If you've bought an iMac you don't have to worry about separate monitors and tower units because it comes in such a tight, all-in-one, space-saving package. In the box you'll have the power cable, along with the wireless mouse/trackpad and wireless keyboard. As with MacBooks, all software is pre-installed on the device.

- **Mac Pro:** Barely anything. You get the unit itself and the power cable. Everything else (keyboard, mouse/trackpad and monitor) is sold separately.

- **Mac Mini:** The Mac Mini is aimed at those who already have a bunch of equipment, so there's little in the box apart from the power cable and a HDMI to DVI adapter for plugging into a HD monitor.

A QUICK TOUR AROUND THE MAC HARDWARE

Now you've got your Mac out of the box, you'll see a host of buttons and connection ports in various positions around the computer. Figuring out what goes where can be quite tricky at first. Here's a helpful guide to what's on show.

Above: MacBook power buttons are top right of the keyboard.

Power Button

No prizes for guessing here. This is how you switch your Mac on, but it can also be used to put the computer to sleep and wake it from hibernation. On MacBooks it appears on the top right of the keyboard. On newer iMacs it's hidden away around the back.

Trackpad

All MacBooks have a rectangular box below the keyboard that's slightly indented into the body. Give it a rub; you'll notice it's slightly smoother than the rest of the casing. This is how you'll navigate around your Mac and select objects on screen. You use a finger to move the cursor or press down to click and make your selection.

Hot Tip

The trackpad is smarter than it looks. It offers a series of multi-touch gestures where you can use more than one digit, pinches, swipes and more to perform different actions.

Trackpad

Ports

Your Mac computer is not an island. To get the most of it, at various times, you'll be plugging in other devices, headphones, power cables, external hard drives, memory cards and so on.

○ **USB 3.0 port**: This is where you'll plug in most of the wired accessories. External hard drives and memory sticks go in here, as do wired mice and keyboards, cameras, smartphones, tablets and sometimes other computers. It's mainly used for transferring data from one device to another, but can also be used to charge your other gadgets.

○ **Thunderbolt**: While not widely used yet, Thunderbolt is the next generation data-transfer technology that features on all new Macs and offers much faster transfers. You can transfer your files up to 20 times faster than when using USB and it'll also play nicely with a new generation of higher-resolution 4K monitors if you need to add a display.

○ **Charging port**: Now this one's pretty essential. MacBook battery life is getting better, but you'll still need to plug in every now and again and iMacs can't run off a battery. On MacBooks the MagSafe adapter magnetically connects, which means if you trip over the cable (as we often do) it'll just pop out without dragging your Mac down with it. On Macs it simply plugs in around the back and stays in, so be careful.

Charging port   Thunderbolt ports   USB 3.0 port   Headphones

○ **Headphones**: There's a 3.5-mm jack on all Macs, where you can plug in your headphones, earphones and portable speakers.

Above: Ports visible on the left side of a MacBook.

○ **Memory card slot**: A feature on the MacBook Pro, MacBook Air (13-in model), iMac, Mac Pro and Mac Mini, it'll allow you to plug in the SD cards that contain your camera's photos or video files. On the MacBook Air 11-in model, you can use a USB adapter to plug in your memory card.

○ **HDMI**: This port, which appears on MacBook Pros and Mac Pros, allows you to connect a high-definition monitor or television with the help of a HDMI cable.

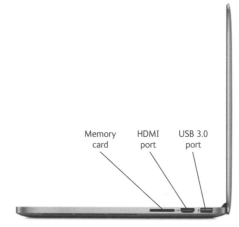

Memory   HDMI   USB 3.0
card   port   port

Above: Ports visible on the right side of a MacBook.

PREPARING YOUR MAC FOR ACTION

We've unboxed your new computer. Now it's ready to be plugged in and prepared for take off.

MacBook

New MacBooks come with enough battery charge to get you started, but you'll want to charge it up ASAP. Pop that MagSafe connector into the slot and (sorry to be obvious) plug the other end into the wall. The light on the connector should turn orange to let you know it's charging. It'll turn green when fully charged. Lift the lid on your laptop and you're pretty much good to go.

Above: The Mac Mini.

iMac

iMacs don't have a portable power source and can only run off the mains. Before switching it on, you'll have to hook up the power cable, which plugs directly into the back of the iMac. Don't worry about the mouse and keyboard. We'll get to that on page 44 in the next chapter.

Mac Pro And Mac Mini

Things are a little different for these machines because of the reliance on other, unbundled accessories. You'll need to hook up the power cable *and* a monitor before you can get started. Most modern monitors will be plugged into the HDMI socket (*see* above). If you're using an existing, wired keyboard and mouse, then plug them into the USB sockets. Wireless peripherals can be set up on start up.

GETTING TO KNOW THE MAC KEYBOARD

There are a few subtle differences that separate the Mac keyboard from the standard keyboard PC users will be used to, but it's easy enough to adjust. Whether it's the keyboard attached to a MacBook or the wireless version that arrives with new iMacs, you'll be shortcutting your way around the keyboard in no time.

1 **Command key:** This is the most important key on the Mac keyboard. Often known as the 'Apple' key, it performs many of the functions of the control key on a PC keyboard, in that it can be combined with others to perform common functions. Command + Q quits a program, Command + S saves a document, while Command + X, C, or V represents cut, copy or paste.

Power button: As referenced earlier in this section, on MacBooks the power button sits in the top right corner of the keyboard.

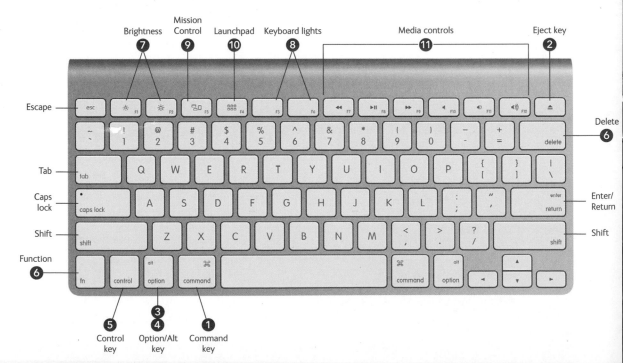

Hot Tip

To close all open
windows in Finder
(*see* page 62),
hit Option +
Command + W.

2 **Eject key:** For iMac, Mac Pro or Mac Mini keyboards, where the device is switched on with a button on the device itself, the button in the top right corner of the keyboard allows for discs to be ejected.

3 **Option key:** A useful yet under-utilized key, this is often combined with other keys, such as Alt, Command and Shift, to perform specific tasks.

4 **Alt keys:** Alt shares a key with Option (they're pretty good friends), and is great for accessing symbols on the keyboard. It's especially good when typing words from foreign languages (Alt + E, then E = é).

5 **Control (ctrl) key:** A lesser used key, but one that comes in handy very occasionally for less essential functions. It's particularly useful in text-editing programs. For example, Control + E moves the cursor to the end of the line.

Hot Tip

For a full list of Mac
keyboard shortcuts – of
which there are too many
to mention here – check out
Apple's official list at
http://support.apple.com
/kb/ht1343

Hot Tip

Lowering screen brightness
is handy when saving
battery or for preventing
your retinas from being
burned out when working
in the dark.

6 **Function (fn) key:** Useless on its own (like Control, Shift, Alt and Option, incidentally), the Function key is used in conjunction with the F-keys on the top row to perform specific actions. They're pre-programmed (for example fn + F9 shows the dashboard) but these features can be customized in System Preferences.

7 **Brightness:** The two keys next to the escape button increase and decrease screen brightness.

8 **Keyboard lights (MacBooks only):** Speaking of working in the dark, the keyboard backlight keys (F5 and F6) can be used to alter the illumination of the keyboard.

9 **Mission Control:** We'll discuss this feature in more detail in Chapter Two, but hitting the icon next to the F3 key activates Mission Control, showing users all open application windows. This feature also sits in the dock.

10 **Launchpad:** Another useful key (F4), this takes you to a screen showing all available apps. This feature is called Launchpad and also sits in the dock.

11 **Media controls:** When playing music or watching video, these keys can be used to play/pause, scan back and forth as well as mute, increase or decrease volume.

12 **Delete:** This one is only slightly confusing. The delete key is effectively backspace when typing. Holding the Function key (fn) will delete words or items in the other direction.

Escape, Caps, Tab, Shift, Enter/Return: In the case of these computing staples, they act in exactly the same way as they do on a PC.

WHAT'S ON THE INSIDE?

Your brand-new Mac is teaming with cutting-edge tech. We've discussed some of it already in the What To Look For section (CPU, RAM, graphics, etc.), but here are some of the other goodies inside your Mac that make the magic happen.

Wi-Fi

Well, you didn't think it connected to the worldwide web by magic, did you? The Wi-Fi chip inside your Mac accepts wireless Internet signals from compatible models, meaning you don't have to plug in to use the Internet.

Bluetooth

Bluetooth is a wireless transfer technology that allows information to be sent over short distances. It's great if you want to chat on a wireless headset, send sound to compatible speakers, or transfer files between other computers and gadgets.

Above: The Wi-Fi and Bluetooth icons sit next to each other on the menu bar.

Microphone

You can barely see this little blighter on most Macs. It lives on the left side of MacBooks and just above the Apple logo on new iMacs. It's tiny but important for any voice-related activity. When chatting on Skype or FaceTime (*see* page 104) the microphone automatically kicks in so your voice can be heard.

Speakers

It's always good to have a decent pair of speakers for playing your music and movie collection. However, before you go out and buy expensive speakers, you should know your Mac has them built in too. They're especially good on the new desktop iMacs.

Webcam

The MacBook Air, MacBook Pro and iMac computers all have the iSight webcam built into the display. You can see it right above the screen. The webcam is capable of snapping stills photos, recording video and transmitting video over the Internet.

Webcam

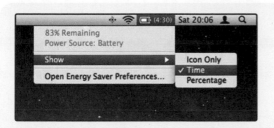

Hot Tip

For longer-lasting battery life, only keep open the apps you're using, and keep the screen brightness at a reasonable level.

Battery (MacBooks Only)

One of the main reasons to plump for a laptop rather than a desktop computer is the ability to use it on the go, perhaps in the park or the back garden, on planes and trains, in coffee shops and libraries, or even on the sofa when you're not close enough to the wall socket. That's made possible by the ever-improving battery cells of MacBooks.

Software

We haven't talked much about software yet. All of that fun stuff will come in the next chapter, but just so you

Above: Mac OS X Mavericks is the latest operating system.

know, the latest version of the Macintosh operating system (at the time of writing, that's Mac OS X Mavericks) is built into your new Mac. If for some reason it's not, then it's a free upgrade, but we'll get to all that stuff. Just know that your Mac is ready to use out of the box.

On that note, let's get started....

GETTING STARTED

POWERING UP AND SETTING UP

Before you get into the nitty gritty of learning to use Mac OS X, you'll need to go through the initial set-up. Everything is extremely straightforward, but this section will guide you through what to click and what not to click.

POWERING UP

Push that button, we know you've been dying to. Almost instantly you'll hear the trademark Apple chime and an Apple logo will appear, backed by a grey screen. In about 30 seconds time you'll be able to get going.

Above: After pressing the Power button, this screen will appear.

Pairing Up The Peripherals (Desktop Macs Only)

Desktop Mac users need to pair up their wireless peripherals before progressing further in the set-up process. Thankfully, with brand-new iMacs the keyboard and trackpad recognise each other from the happy time they spent together at the Mac factory.

1. On the initial start-up screen the Mac will request that you turn on your wireless mouse or trackpad and the two should sync up almost immediately.

2. Move your cursor and click the arrow to continue past the welcome screen.

3. Next it'll ask you to turn on the wireless keyboard. Hit the button on the side of the accessory and a green light will start flashing and the two should pair up in a few seconds.

Hot Tip

USB peripherals, should they be Mac compatible, will be recognized instantly.

Choosing Your Region And Keyboard Layout

This is your Mac's way of asking: 'Where you at?' Firstly, you need to select your location from the list of countries in the drop-down menu, then hit Continue. The next screen asks you to select the keyboard language. Make sure you choose English US or UK, depending on your preferences, as there are some subtle differences.

Connecting To Your Network

Next, your new Mac will ask you to select a Wi-Fi network. If you have an Internet connection at home, then this shouldn't be too stressful. Select your network ID from the list of in-range connections (it'll be printed on a sticker on your broadband modem), then type in the password (also printed on the sticker) on your newly connected keyboard and hit Continue.

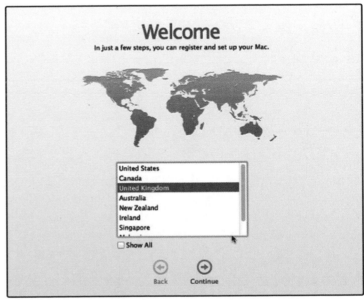

Above: Select the correct country from the drop-down menu.

Wired Network (Ethernet)

If you wish to use a wired connection, plug in an Ethernet cable and select the Other Network Options button on the Wi-Fi screen. Then select Local Network (Ethernet) from the options and follow the on-screen instructions. See the chapter on Networking (pages 152–181) for more detailed information.

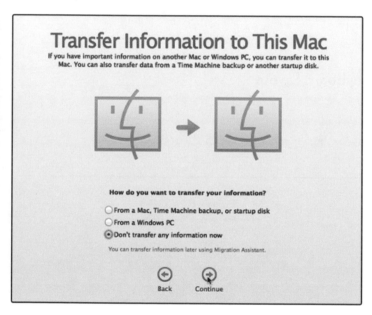

Above: It is easy to transfer files from another or computer or disc on to your Mac.

Transferring Your Data?

In recent versions of the Mac OS X software, users are able to transfer all of their files over from other computers they have. This is great if you're a Windows user transferring over to Mac for the first time.

The options are From Another Mac, From A Windows PC or From Another Disc. We'll discuss this in more detail later, as it's something that can be done at a later date using the Migration Assistant. For our purposes, hit Not Now and continue.

Location Services

Your Mac contains a GPS chip that can determine your approximate location. This comes in handy when performing Internet searches for something

Hot Tip

At any point in the set-up you can hit the Back arrow to alter any information. Likewise, nothing you input during set-up is set in stone. It can all be amended later.

like movie screening times, restaurants in your vicinity, or directions using a service like Apple Maps. To allow Location Services, click the tick box and press Continue.

Entering Your Apple ID

Do you own an iPhone, iPad or iPod touch? Then you will most likely have an Apple ID account. It can be used on Macs to set up the iTunes Store, the Mac App Store and the iCloud back-up service. If you have one, but don't want to set it up yet, you can skip this step.

1. If you have an Apple ID, enter the email and password associated with the account and hit Continue.

2. If you wish to use a different Apple ID for iCloud and iTunes, then hit that option to configure settings.

3. You can also recover your password or ID, if you've forgotten either or both using this screen.

Above: If you already have an Apple ID, simply enter your email address and password.

The Paperwork

Next, you'll need to accept some of those pesky terms and conditions. There's no way around it. Hardly anyone ever reads these, but you can click the various services (iCloud, Game Center, iTunes, etc.) to see exactly what you're agreeing to, or just blindly accept by hitting the tick box and then Agree.

Above: Enable iCloud in order to sync various applications.

Connecting With The iCloud

If you've entered your Apple ID (see above), you'll have the opportunity to configure your Mac with iCloud. This means you'll be able to sync things like email, documents, Internet bookmarks, notes and contacts. If you want to enable iCloud from the get-go, click Continue a couple of times.

Getting The iMessage Out

The next screen allows you to configure the accounts at which users can reach you through the Messages chat app and the FaceTime video chat service. Macs running newer versions of OS X can send and receive free SMS messages from others using an Apple device, either through the Mac, iPhone, iPod touch or iPad. All of those messages sync back to all devices, thanks to iCloud.

If you've agreed to iCloud, all of the email accounts/phone numbers already associated with that Apple ID will appear and you can tick/untick those you'd like to use. Once you're happy, click Continue.

Keeping Tabs On Your Mac

Don't worry, just a few more screens to go. Here you'll need to decide whether you'd like

Hot Tip

You can use Find My Mac to lock or wipe all of your computer's contents remotely, preventing your sensitive data or photos getting into the wrong hands.

to use iCloud to track your Mac's location. Should your computer be mislaid or stolen, you can log into iCloud.com and use the Find My Mac service to track its location. It'll even play a sound if you've mislaid it in your home!

Creating Your Computer Account

Even if you don't feel like using Find Your Mac, you definitely need to create a password for your computer to keep potential intruders out. On this screen you input your name, choose a name for your computer's Home file and, most importantly, add a password. Try to choose something that's easy for you to remember, but something no one else will guess. Don't use your name or date of birth!

Pick Your Pic

The account screen also allows you to customize your Mac with a profile picture. By clicking the square box next to the name, the Photo Booth camera interface will load and you can take what the kids refer to as a 'selfie' using the webcam. This can be changed with a fancier pic at a later time.

Create a Computer Account
Fill out the following information to create your computer account.

Full name: Christopher J Smith
Account name: chrissmith
This will be the name of your home folder.
Password: ••••••   ••••••
Hint: optional
☑ Require password to unlock screen
☑ Allow my Apple ID to reset this password
Options: ☑ Set time zone based on current location
☑ Send Diagnostics & Usage data to Apple
Help Apple improve its products and services by automatically and periodically sending diagnostic and usage data. About Diagnostics and Privacy...

Creating account...   Back   Continue

Above: Choose a password which will be difficult for others to guess, e.g. not your date of birth.

Hot Tip
Make sure the 'Require password when logging in' checkbox is ticked. The password will also be used to change settings, install software and administer your computer, so make it a good one.

Above: Load the Photo Booth interface and take a photo of yourself to use as your profile picture.

In The (Time) Zone

Nearly there! One of your final set-up actions is to select your computer's time zone. You can either hit the automatic location tick box or click your location on the map in order to keep your clock and calendar functioning accurately. As an added bonus, it will also automatically update when the clocks change.

To Register Or Not To Register?

On this screen Apple asks you for your postal and email addresses in order to get faster access to support. This isn't entirely necessary, so you can skip for now if you wish.

Step Up Is Complete!

Woo and indeed hoo! The next screen congratulates you on navigating the set-up minefield. Do yourself a favour: click that button that says 'Start using your Mac'. Welcome to your brand-new Apple Mac. Let's get started.

A CLOSER LOOK AT MAC OS X

Once set-up is complete you'll be taken straight to your Mac's desktop. Every function on your Mac computer can be accessed from this point in some way, shape or form.

WHAT IS MAC OS X?

As we alluded to in the previous chapter, the software you now see before your eyes is called Mac OS X. It's made by Apple for Apple computers. Simple as that. If you're using a brand-new Mac it is extremely likely that you're using version 10.9, which is known as Mavericks.

Above: The Mac OS X desktop has a sleek design.

Which Version Of Mac OS X Are You Using?

Apple introduced OS X (the tenth version of its computing operating system) as a pre-loaded feature of all Macs in 2002 and it's been a staple ever since. Every year (or so) it gets a fresh lick of paint with some new features. Here's a brief guide to the last few releases.

- **OS X 10.9 Mavericks (2013):** The first free upgrade for Mac users brought a new Maps app, access to ebooks through the iBooks store and more.

- **OS X 10.8 Mountain Lion (2012):** Borrowed features from the iPhone and iPad such as Reminders, Messages, Notification Center and Game Center.

- **OS X 10.7 Lion (2011):** The introduction of Mission Control, Launchpad and multi-touch gestures on the trackpad.

- **OS X 10.6 Snow Leopard (2009):** Mainly under-the-hood changes to improve performance and efficiency, but it did mark the debut of the Mac App Store (*see* page 131).

- **OS X 10.5 Leopard (2007):** 300 new features included the introduction of Time Machine (*see* page 188) and a revamped Finder.

Upgrading To Mavericks

If you're using a slightly older Mac and want the latest and greatest software features, then you can upgrade to OS X Mavericks free of charge. It's available to Macs running OS X 10.6 Snow Leopard and above. You can see compatible models here: http://www.apple.com/osx/how-to-upgrade/. If you're good to go, let's get you bang up to date.

1. Make sure your data is backed up first. While software updates don't often cause problems, it's better to be safe than sorry (*see* page 184).

2. Select the Apple logo and click Software Update...

Above: If your Mac is compatible with OS X Mavericks software, it doesn't cost anything to upgrade to it.

3. Browse to Updates and you'll see OS X Mavericks sitting right there.

4. Simply go through the install process and follow the on-screen steps.

5. You'll be running OS X Mavericks in no time at all.

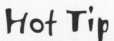

If you're not sure which version of Mac OS X your computer is running, hit the Apple logo in the menu bar and select About This Mac.

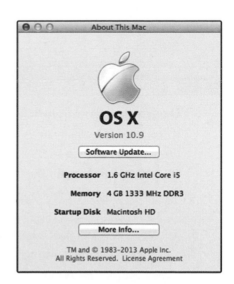

Above: About This Mac offers key system information.

MAC OS X BASICS

We're guessing you've had enough of the history lesson and set-up stuff by now. In front of you is a blank desktop canvas waiting to be filled and a dock full of apps waiting to be put to use. Without further ado, let's do some exploring.

Above: Click the Finder icon on the dock to bring up a Finder window, and access your files.

THE BIG FOUR

Once start-up is complete, you'll see the Mac OS X desktop. At this stage it's probably easier to split the general user interface into four sections. There's the desktop, which dominates most of the Mac's display, the dock at the bottom of the screen and the menu bar at the top of the screen. There's also the Finder functionality, which is the closest thing to the Windows start button you'll see on a Mac. Before we go into detail, let's introduce all four.

The Desktop

Right now the majority of the display is covered only with the Mac OS X wallpaper, but pretty soon you'll be

Hot Tip

To see all open app windows on the screen, hit the Mission Control button on your keyboard (F3). Move the cursor to the app of your choice and click.

loading up the desktop with files, folders, photos, software and more. Naturally, when any apps are open they appear within this space, layered on top of each other depending on which you're using.

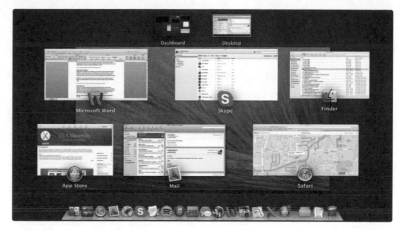

Above: Press F3 on the keyboard to bring up Mission Control. This shows you all open apps.

Finder

Finder is a very important part of the Mac OS X experience. As the name suggests, the Finder window offers fast access to everything on your computer. Opening a Finder window offers fast access to every file, folder, application and programme. When you're working on the desktop, you're already in Finder mode, while clicking the Finder icon in the dock brings up a window.

Above: The Finder function offers a fast way to access your applications and files.

Hot Tip

When working on the desktop hit Control + N to open a new Finder window.

Above: Save your most commonly used programs to the dock for quick access to them.

The Dock

The Mac OS X dock is awesome and a signature of the user interface. It's a home for all of your favourite programs and represents a simple way to open and switch between all of your software. If an app is open, its icon sits neatly in the dock. Go ahead, move your cursor over one of the application icons and click it; it won't bite!

Above: The menu bar hosts both features for the currently open app and general information.

The Menu Bar

The translucent bar at the very top of the screen features commands for the app you're currently using. For example, for Mail you'll see the name of the program next to the Apple logo, followed by File, Edit, View and all that good stuff. However, there's also a host of static icons at the right edge of the screen, which inform you about battery life, Internet status, the time and more. Tap these menu items for more options.

NAVIGATION BASICS

Here are a few basic skills you'll need to master, along with some tips to help you master the keyboard, mouse and trackpad.

USING THE MOUSE OR TRACKPAD

Without a mouse or trackpad it's nigh on impossible to do anything with your new Mac. Go on, try it and see how far you get. Moving the mouse with your hand or moving around the trackpad by lightly pressing down and dragging a finger, moves the cursor in the desired direction.

Clicking And Right Clicking

Whether you're using a traditional mouse, a Magic Trackpad or a laptop trackpad, you can push down to click and select the option your cursor is hovering over. The act of 'right clicking' traditionally accesses options within specific apps (if you right click an app in the dock, you can quit it), but you'll notice there's no 'right' button on the Mac mouse or trackpad as there is on a Windows PC. To get around this you can a) click the trackpad with two fingers rather than one or b) hold the Control button as you click the mouse or trackpad.

Above: One method of right-clicking on an icon is to hold the Control button as you click the trackpad or mouse.

Dragging And Dropping

If you want to move items around your Mac, dragging and dropping is an important tool. For example, if you pick up a song file, drag it and drop it on to the iTunes icon within the dock, and that song will open in iTunes and begin playing. If you drag a file on to the trash bucket within the dock and drop it, it will be placed in the Trash.

To drag and drop, click on a file and hold down the mouse or trackpad button. With the button still held down, move the mouse or use a different finger to move the trackpad to the new destination and release the mouse and trackpad. Simple.

Above: To delete a file, use the drag and drop method to select the file and move it into the Trash.

Keyboard Shortcuts

You can perform a lot of popular tasks on your Mac by performing simple keyboard shortcuts. A keyboard shortcut is achieved by hitting a combination of two or more keys at the same time. We'll mention many of these as we go along, but here are some of the simplest and most commonly used. Remember they perform differently within different apps.

Command + A = Select all items within a window
Command + B = Make selected text bold in documents
Command + C = Copy all selected items to the clipboard
Command + D = Add a bookmark when using Internet browsers
Command + E = Eject a CD or DVD
Command + F = Access the search box within a given app (F = find!)
Command + I = Get information about a file or folder/Make selected text italic in documents
Command + M = Minimize a window
Command + N = New document, new file, new window, new playlist, etc.
Command + O − Open a file
Command + P = Print
Command + Q = Quit a program
Command + R = Refresh a webpage
Command + S = Save
Command + T = Open a new tab in Finder
or in the web browser
Command + U = Underline selected text
within documents
Command + V = Paste selected items
Command + W = Close the current window
Command + X = Cut selected items
Command + Z = Undo the last action

Some of the more complex actions require more than two keys. For example:
Command + Option + Esc   = Force Quit app menu
Command + Option + Mac = Minimize all windows within an app
Command + Shift + 3   = Take a screenshot

USING THE DOCK

As we mentioned previously, the dock is one of your best friends on the Mac. From set-up it is jam-packed across the board with Apple's stock applications. Here you'll find things like Finder, Mail, the Safari web browser, iTunes and the App Store.

Above: As you hover over an icon in the dock it will magnify and its name will appear.

Opening Apps In The Dock

This is the easy part. Move the cursor down to a particular icon in the dock such as the compass, which represents the Safari web browser. As you hover over the icon you'll see the icon will magnify slightly and the app's name appear in a speech bubble. Simply click the icon with your mouse or trackpad.

If the app is already open, it'll bring that window to the forefront of the display. If the app is closed, the icon will begin to bounce and open the app in at the point it was last closed.

Customizing The Dock

As you get to know your Mac you'll want to make the dock more efficient. That means ditching the programs you don't use and adding the ones you use a lot. You can also change the size, visibility and position of the dock. Here's how.

Hot Tip

You can tell which apps in the Dock are open by the presence of a light indicator underneath the icon.

1. To keep an open app in the dock at all times, right click the icon within the dock and select Options, then Keep in Dock.

2. To remove an app from the dock, right click the icon, select Options and untick Keep in Dock. Alternatively, grab the app icon, drag it out of the dock and release. It'll disappear in a puff of smoke.

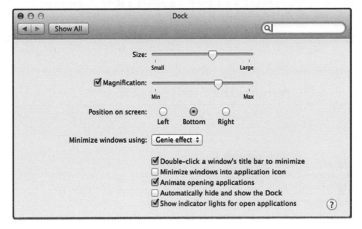

Step 5: Alter the size of the icon when magnified by sliding between Min and Max.

3. You can also hide the dock from constant view so it only appears when you move the cursor to the very bottom of the screen. This can be handy to ensure it doesn't interfere with other apps. Head to System Preferences, select Dock and then tick Automatically hide and show the Dock.

4. To alter the size of the dock, enter System Preferences, select Dock and pull the scroll bar left or right to make it smaller or larger.

5. To alter the scale of the magnification when the cursor hovers over apps, enter System Preferences > Dock and drag the scroll bar towards Min or Max. You can even untick the box to turn magnification off.

6. If you don't like the dock at the bottom of the screen you can move it to the left or right by selecting a Position on screen button within the dock preferences.

Step 6: The dock does not have to run along the bottom of the screen; it can be moved to the side.

WORKING WITH FINDER

Finder is an essential navigation tool when looking for files, apps and folders within your Mac. Think of it as your command centre. Here's how to master it.

Opening The Finder Window

There are a couple of ways to access and open a Finder window on your Mac. The easiest is to head to the dock and click the first icon, which looks like two smiley blue faces. That'll immediately open an existing Finder window, or begin a new one. If you're working on the desktop, Finder is the default app that appears in the menu bar. You can either hit Command + N to open a new window or File > New Finder Window.

Above: The Finder window has a sidebar with access to favourite items.

Touring The Finder Window

Okay, there's plenty to see here so let's take things slowly and talk through each of the relevant sections, starting with the Favourites sidebar. Hitting one of the options within the sidebar will populate the adjacent section. From here you can use the mouse and trackpad to scan and select files.

- **All My Files:** The default view in Finder is the All My Files section, which shows every single folder on your computer, starting with the most recent. This is handy if you're looking for recently accessed or downloaded files.

- **AirDrop:** More on this in Chapter Five, but simply put AirDrop allows you to send and receive files from other close-by Macs.

○ **Desktop**: Shows a list of all files saved to your desktop.

○ **Documents**: Everything you have saved within your Mac's Docments folder.

○ **Downloads**: This is helpful when you've obtained files from online sources. Unless you've specified otherwise, they'll be saved in this folder.

○ **Movies and Music**: These two options give access to your media files.

Hot Tip

To control what appears in the Favourites sidebar, hit Finder in the menu bar followed by Preferences and Sidebar to tick/untick items.

○ **Applications**: You'll probably use this one a lot. It's a shortcut to a list of applications you have installed on your Mac.

○ **Pictures**: Your iPhoto library and other pictures are saved to this default folder.

○ **Home**: The home folder is usually named after your computer's account and also features a progressive path to items on your computer.

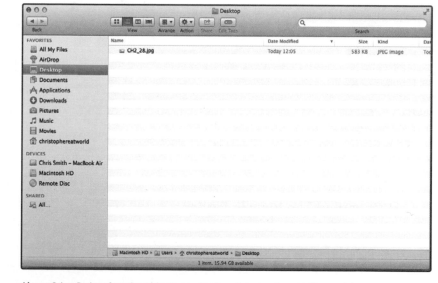

Above: Select Desktop from the sidebar to populate the adjacent section with files saved there.

Above: Quick Look allows you to preview a file without opening the app.

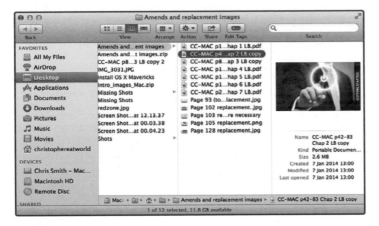

Above: The column view in Finder can make it easier to browse between folders.

Quick Look

Quick Look, the eye icon within the Finder window toolbar, is a very useful feature. Selecting a file (or multiple files) and hitting Quick Look will immediately show a preview of each file, without the need to open the full app. This is very useful if you need a closer look than the thumbnail. From here you can share the file via Mail, Messages and others, or open it in another app.

Back And Forth

As you progress through the file and folder paths in Finder, sometimes you'll need to backtrack to the previous screen. This is enabled by the useful arrows in the Finder window.

Changing The View In Finder

The window also boasts a view section allowing users to choose how the files appear. Hitting these icons allows you to view thumbnails (useful for photographs), files in a long list (useful when looking for documents), files in column view (opening up the file path) and as Cover Flow, which shows thumbnails that can easily be whizzed through.

Deleting Files Using Finder

The view offered within the Finder window makes it easy to delete unwanted files your Mac. If, for example, you're looking through the Downloads folder, you can select those you wish to delete and then hit the trashcan icon in the Finder window. This will move those files to the Trash, which you'll see within the dock.

Selecting Multiple Files

Sometimes you'll want to open/share more than one file at a time. Instead of clicking all of those files individually, you can batch them together and perform the task in one fell swoop. Here's how.

1. To select more than one file: Click the file of your choice, then hold down the Shift key and click the last item in the list you wish to select. This will group them all together and highlight them in blue.

2. To pick and choose the items you wish to select, pick one file and hold down the Command key and click each one individually.

3. From here you can right click on one of the files, or hit the Action icon in the Finder window and choose the group action. Perhaps it's Open, Open With (a particular app), Share or creating a new folder.

Step 3: Once the files are selected, right click and select the action you want to perform to all.

Moving Files Around In Finder

To prevent your Mac becoming a big unorganized mess of files and programs, you'll need to do a bit of organizing here and there, grouping things together in specially created folders or moving items from one folder to another.

1. To create a new folder within a Finder window use the shortcut Command + Shift + N. It'll appear under the name 'untitled folder'. You can just start typing and then hit enter to give it a name.

2. To move items into the folder, select the files in question (see above) and drag and drop them into the newly created folder.

Hot Tip
To move easily between tabs, use the keyboard shortcut Command + Tab.

3. You can also drag and drop selected files into Trash, on to an application icon within the dock to open them in that app, or move them to any of the Favourites folders listed in the sidebar, for example, the Documents folder.

Above: Finder windows can have multiple tabs, so no need for several Finder windows.

Finder Tabs In OS X Mavericks

One of the helpful new features introduced within Mac OS X Mavericks was Finder tabs. This means you don't have to have multiple Finder windows all over the place. To open a Finder tab use the keyboard shortcut Command + T. Additional tabs can be opened using the '+' icon in the top right corner of the window.

Searching Using Finder

Well it wouldn't be a very good Finder if it didn't allow you to search, right? Thankfully, within the window there's a box dedicated to finding what you need by name. Move your cursor into the box and start typing. This will immediately show files, folders and apps with matching names on your Mac. Also listed is the folder within which you began the search. Hit this to narrow down the results.

Sharing Using Finder

The Finder also represents an easy way for you to share files and folders with others. Once a file is selected within a window, you can hit the Share icon in the toolbar, which presents available options. For example, photos can be shared via Mail (opens a new email message complete with the attached file), Messages (likewise) or through Facebook and Twitter (if you have those accounts linked up).

Above: Select a file and then click the Share icon at the top of the Finder window.

Customizing The Finder Window

Like most things on a Mac, the Finder window itself can be customized to look exactly how you wish, adding or subtracting items for personal preference. For example, if you right click on the toolbar you'll see the Customise Toolbar option appear.

Selecting this option presents a menu packed full of icons that can be dragged and dropped (see page 58) directly on to the toolbar. Say, for example, Get Info, which you can press in order to learn more about a selected file, it can be pinned to the toolbar.

WORKING WITH THE MENU BAR

The menu bar sits across the top of the display at all times and offers application-specific commands as well as a host of information about the key functions of your Mac. Hitting each of the items in the menu bar opens a drop-down menu, allowing you to select relevant actions.

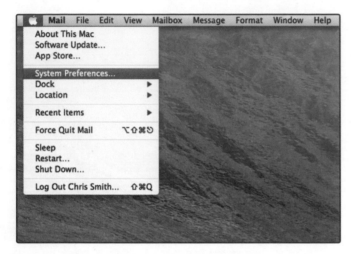

Above: The Apple logo provides access to key functions on your Mac.

Apple Logo

One thing that's always there is the Apple logo in the top left corner. Beneath this button, you'll have a shortcut to a few of your Mac's key functions. You can open the System Preferences app to modify your settings, access the App Store and Software Updates, open recent documents and, if the work or play is done for the day, you can choose to put your computer to sleep, restart it or shut it down completely.

It's All In The Name

If you have lots of windows open, it's easy to lose track of which app you're currently controlling. This is solved by a quick look to the top left of the menu bar. For example, as I type this document, my Mac says 'Word'. From this menu, you can access the app-specific preferences and quit the program.

Other Headers In The Menu Bar

As we mentioned above, the other headers vary depending on the app you're working with at the time. Here are some of the most common.

- **File:** Here you can create new items, open existing items, save, share, print and more.

● **Edit**: Another common header in most apps in Mac OS X. Here you'll be able to cut, copy and paste selected items, as well as access the undo last step and redo features.

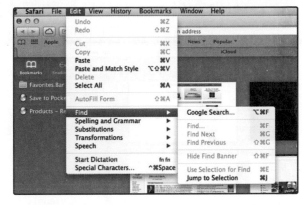

● **View**: View generally controls the appearance of the application; what you see and what you don't. For example, in the Safari web browser, you can View > Show/Hide Sidebar.

Above: The Edit menu allows you to copy and paste amongst other functions.

● **Window**: This function can be used to minimize or maximize particular windows or to choose which window to bring to the front of the screen.

● **Help**: Help is ever present. Here you can type in questions and you'll mostly be presented with easy-to-understand answers.

HOW THE OTHER HALF (of the Menu Bar) LIVES

While the left side offers access to app-specific tools, the icons to the right are always present, irrespective of which app you're in. They show connectivity status, remaining battery life, the time and much more. Here they are, from right to left.

Above: Icons on the right hand side of the menu are not specific to whichever app is open, but give more general information.

Stay Notified

We'll talk more about Notifications in the next chapter, but the list-like icon you'll see within the menu bar is how you access them. Opening this reveals a sidebar on your Mac showing recent emails, messages, forthcoming calendar appointments and social-networking tools. From here you can also control which notifications you receive and how they appear on screen.

Above: Click the magnifying glass icon to search your Mac.

Putting Your Files In The Spotlight

Spotlight has been an integral part of Mac OS X since its inception and is the easiest way to find absolutely anything on your Mac, whether it's an app or a file or even a key word within emails, messages or documents. Just hit the magnifying glass and start typing and results will immediately begin populating below.

[Your Name Goes Here]

Most of the time, your name will sit next to the Spotlight magnifying glass. This is to let you know which account is in use. Macs can have multiple user accounts for both security and convenience. Clicking the name allows users to switch between accounts from the drop-down menu.

Hot Tip

When charging, click the battery icon and you'll receive an estimate of how long it'll be until it is fully charged.

Keeping Track Of Time

Do you ever get so absorbed in creating that office PowerPoint presentation that you lose all track of time and space? No, us neither, but having a clock there sure does help sometimes. Clicking the clock will also show you the date.

Battery Life

iMac, Mac Mini and Mac Pro users can skip this bit, but for MacBook users this is probably the most crucial part of the menu bar. When the battery is off charge you'll see a percentage of how much is left. When it gets into the red, you've got less than 10 per cent left and you'll need to plug in. When plugged in, the reading will still show the remaining battery life.

Volume Rocker

There are a couple of ways you can adjust the system volume on your trusty Mac. One is with the on-keyboard buttons (F10/F11/F12), the other is with the slider in the menu bar. Hit this and drag the volume up and down. There's a visual representation of the current volume at all times.

Are You Online?

This icon is pretty crucial too as it shows your Internet connectivity status. If the signal bar is full, it means you're online and have great signal. The bars will drop if you're connected to a network, but have a weaker signal.

If you're offline, the bars meter will be empty, while if you're unable to connect to a network an exclamation point will appear in the meter. If Wi-Fi is turned off, you'll see a hollow meter.

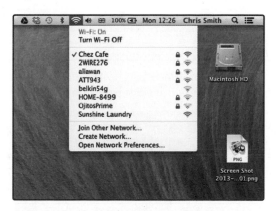

Above: Click this icon to check the Internet connectivity status of the Mac.

If you click the Internet meter, you can choose to join a different network from the drop-down menu, turn Wi-Fi on and off (this is sometimes helpful if you briefly lose connectivity), and also access Network Preferences.

Other Menu Bar Items

You can put anything you want to in the menu bar. Apps like Skype also make their presence known when in use. You'll also see icons for modifying AirPlay, Time Machine and Bluetooth settings. There'll be more on these throughout the book.

Hot Tip

Your Mac has a great memory and remembers every place where you've connected to a Wi-Fi network. Next time you visit that place you'll automatically be connected to that network.

WORKING WITH YOUR DESKTOP

The desktop is useful as a place to store files and folders that don't necessarily have an immediate home, such as email attachments, new documents and anything that you'd like to have at hand without delving through the file paths.

Organizing Your Desktop

The desktop can get quite messy from time to time, but there are plenty of ways to bring some order to the chaos, by arranging the icons. Right click on an available area of the desktop and hit Clean Up By or Sort By to arrange the icons by Name, Date, Size, Last Opened or More.

Hot Tip

To access your desktop at any time without minimizing or closing your app windows set up a Hot Corner (*see* page 75).

Above: Right click on the desktop and select Clean Up By in order to organise the files on the desktop.

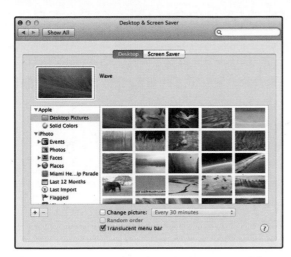

Above: Personalize the desktop background with your picture of choice.

Changing The Desktop Background

The default wallpaper that ships with Mac OS X is lovely and all, but we'd prefer a picture of our mother's dog. To change the desktop background, right click on a free part of the desktop and choose – you guessed it – Change Desktop Background. Here you can select from the default options or use one of your own photos.

View Options

You can also customize the size of the file icons, and whether text and information is shown alongside them by right clicking and hitting Show View Options and playing with the settings.

Saving To Desktop

Whenever you're saving a file, be it an email attachment, a Word document or a photo, you'll often be asked where you'd like to save it. If you'd like to dump it on the desktop for convenience, just use the Command + D keyboard shortcut when within the Save dialogue box.

Above: To save an item to the desktop, press Command + D within the Save dialogue box.

MULTI-TOUCH GESTURES AND HOT CORNERS

These two pieces of Mac OS X functionality are part of what makes using Macs so enjoyable. With a simple swipe or pinch on the trackpad or by moving the cursor into one of the four corners you can perform actions more easily than ever.

Above: Trackpad preferences offers descriptions of available gestures.

Getting Used To Multi-touch

Inspired by the touch screen gestures on the iPhone and iPad, multi-touch gestures on Mac computers add functionality to the trackpad, using two or more fingers to perform certain actions. Apple offers a neat description and animations of available gestures at System Preferences > Trackpad, but here are some of our most used gestures.

○ **Two fingers in any direction**: Scroll around individual windows and documents. The movement follows your fingers and means you don't have to use in-app scroll bars.

○ **Swipe left or right with three fingers**: Move between full-screen apps or access the dashboard (*see* page 119).

○ **Pinch with two fingers**: Zoom in or out on photos and other items.

○ **Swipe down with three fingers**: Access App Exposé, which shows all open windows within an app, allowing you to easily move between them.

○ **Swipe up with three fingers**: Access Mission Control, showing all open apps left or right with two fingers: move between pages in a window. Can be a handy alternative to the back/forward arrows.

Note: Gestures can be customized and are slightly different when using a Magic Mouse rather than a trackpad

Mastering Hot Corners

Hot Corners are a great way of getting around your Mac quickly, just by moving the cursor into one of the four corners of the display. You can customize them in whichever way you see fit.

1. Go to System Preferences > Mission Control > Hot Corners. You'll see a new window with four pull-down menus, one for each corner.

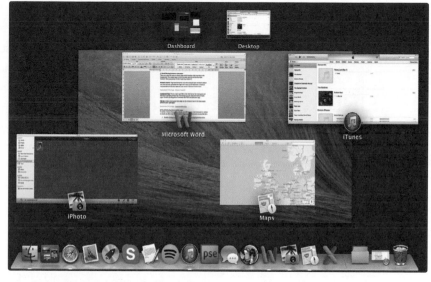

2. Select from any of the 9 actions for each Hot Corner. Your options are:

Above: Select Application Windows for one of your Hot Corner actions and you will be able to see all current open applications.

- ○ Access **Mission Control** (see page 77)
- ○ Show open **Application Windows**
- ○ Show **Desktop**
- ○ Show **Dashboard**
- ○ Show **Notification Center**

- ○ Show **Launchpad**
- ○ **Start Screen Saver**
- ○ **Disable Screen Saver**
- ○ **Put Display to Sleep**

3. To return to the previous stage, just revisit the same corner.

We find Desktop and Application Windows by far the most useful Hot Corners, but it'll vary for each user.

APPLICATION BASICS

You're now familiar with the most essential user-interface tools in your Mac's arsenal, but it's difficult to work or play unless you're familiar with how to use the computer's suite of applications. In this section, we'll show you how to find, open and close your apps.

FINDING AND OPENING APPS

There are a number of ways to browse your Mac's applications, some of which we've already discussed within this chapter.

Hot Tip

To place an Applications folder shortcut in the dock, head to Finder > Applications sidebar > right click and Add to Dock. Click the shortcut and select the icon of your choosing to open.

1. The easiest way is to navigate to them within the dock (*see* page 60). Click an app to open.

2. Use the Finder > Applications sidebar to see a list of everything that's installed. Double click to open one.

Above: From the Launchpad screen you will see a grid of apps. You can then easily select the app you want.

Launchpad

Launchpad, as the name would suggest, is an area of your Mac where every app sits. Hit the space rocket icon in the dock, press **F4** on the keyboard or move the cursor into a configured Hot Corner and you'll see a new screen that looks a little like the iPad's layout with a grid of apps. Simply hit the app of your choice to open.

Moving Between Open Apps

There are a few fun ways to switch apps while keeping others running in the background. The easiest way is to hit the open app icon within the dock. However, there are plenty of other ways to go about it.

Mission Control: Represented by the icon with multiple open windows within the dock and also accessible through

Hot Tip

Create a Hot Corner (see page 75) for Mission Control for even easier access to your open apps.

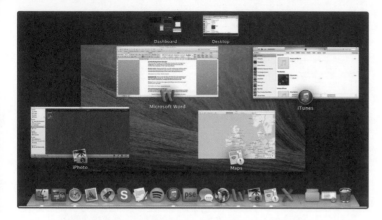

the F3 key on the keyboard. It shows a representation of all open apps on your screen. Click on one to move to it.

Command + Shift + Tab: This is a neat little trick. Hold down the Command and Shift keys together and tap Tab. This brings up an on-screen menu of open apps. Continue holding down Command and Shift and pick your app.

Above: Press F3 or click the icon on the dock with multiple open windows to bring up Mission Control. This will display all open apps.

Above: Hold down Command and Shift, then tap Tab. Keep holding Command and Shift, then select an icon from the menu of open apps.

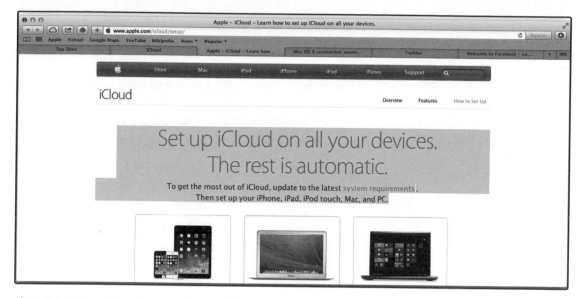

Above: To highlight a selection of text on a webpage, hold down and drag the trackpad or mouse over the area.

Selecting Items Within Apps

To select a block of text on a webpage, in a URL bar, in a text document or within an email, you first need to highlight it. There are several ways to do this.

1. Double clicking a word highlights it, a triple click highlights the entire paragraph or line.

2. Command + A selects everything within the window.

3. Holding down on the mouse or trackpad and using it to move over the area you wish to select, allows you to highlight that area.

Once the section is highlighted, Command + C copies the text, Command + X cuts it and Command + V pastes it within an email, document or app. Right clicking serves up a wider array of options, such as the dictionary or formatting options.

MOVING, MINIMIZING, MAXIMIZING, RESIZING

There's plenty you can do to customise your in-app experience.

Minimizing Apps And Windows

To hide a window from view, you can hit the Command + M keyboard shortcut. You'll see a neat genie-in-a-bottle effect as the window descends into the dock. Alternatively, you can hit the amber circle in the top left corner of the window. You can summon it once again by finding it in the dock.

Maximizing Apps

To extend a window so all content is viewable on the horizontal axis, click the green '+' icon in the top left corner of the window. To ensure it fills the screen, hold down the shift key as you hit the icon.

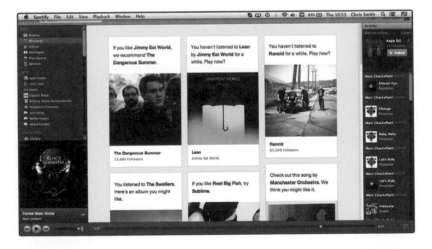

Resizing Windows

You can easily customize how your app windows appear on screen, by placing the cursor in the bottom right corner, holding down the mouse or trackpad and dragging to the new size.

Left: Making apps full screen allows you to focus solely on the current task..

Moving Windows

You can easily move the Windows around the display (or to a different display) by dragging the title bar around the screen.

Going Full Screen

Mac OS X now has a neat full-screen mode, which aids productivity by allowing your current app to completely fill the screen. Hit the arrows in the top right corner of the window. Exit by sending the cursor to menu bar and hitting the blue arrows.

Closing Windows

To get rid of a tab or an individual window within an app, there's a simple keyboard shortcut – Command + W. In some apps, if there are unsaved changes you'll be asked to save before it closes. You can also hit the red circle within the window itself to close the window.

Quitting Apps

Having apps open when you're not using them not only adds to the clutter on your screen, but it also drains system memory, slowing your computer's performance and, if you're using a MacBook, adds to battery drain. Here's how to shut them down.

1. Hold down the Command key and hit Q to shut down the app in question. If you're working on a project, you'll be asked to save your progress before you quit.

Hot Tip

When apps are in full-screen mode, you can move between them by swiping three fingers across the trackpad left and right. For more multi-touch gestures, *see page 74*.

Hot Tip

Command + Option + Control + Media Eject (power button on MacBooks) forces all programs to quit, while giving you the opportunity to save progress in each.

Step 4: Press Command + Alt + Escape to Force Quit programs.

2. Hit the application name in the menu bar and select Quit.

3. Right click on the app in the dock and hit Quit.

4. You can Force Quit applications (great if they're not responding to you through conventional means) by hitting Command + Alt + Escape. Then you can close apps individually. Beware, unsaved progress will be lost if using Force Quit (see image on page 81).

Resuming Apps

Apple Mac OS X has a great Resume feature, which allows you to pick up where you left off in some apps. For example, if you quit Text Edit, Pages or Safari without closing individual windows, those windows and tabs will appear again when you re-open the app.

WHEN YOU'RE NOT USING YOUR MAC

As much as we love using our Mac, it's wise to take a break every now and again. Here are your options when you're ready to pack up for the day, or need to restart your computer.

Sleep Mode

While it's wise to give your Mac a complete break by shutting down or giving it a 'power cycle' every now and again, you can mostly get away with putting your Mac to sleep. This is an extremely low-power mode that preserves all of the apps you're working on without putting strain on the battery or using as much electricity.

1. If you're a MacBook owner simply close the lid to put your device to sleep.

2. Tap the power button once (in OS X Mavericks).

3. Select the Apple logo in the menu bar and hit Sleep.

To wake your Mac from its snooze, you can simply open the lid on a MacBook, hit any key on the keyboard or tap the power button once again. You'll need to log back in using your computer's password.

Restarting Your Mac

There are plenty of occasions where it makes sense to restart your Mac. It can be necessary to complete program installations, it can offer a quick fix for many ills, and it's also good to start with a clean slate every once in a while. Once the restart is complete, log back into your computer and you're good to go again.

1. The easiest way is to hit the Apple logo and scroll down to restart. You'll be asked to save progress in apps as each one closes.

2. To force the instant restart of the computer, hit the Command + Control + Media Eject (power button).

3. Alternatively, hit Control + Media Eject (power button) to show the Restart/Sleep/Shut Down dialogue box.

Above: Hit Control + Media Eject to show the Restart/Sleep/Shut Down options.

Shutting Down

Other than a pint of your local's finest ale, there's no better way to underscore a working day than shutting down your Mac for the day. The methods are very similar to Sleep and Restart.

1. Hit the Apple logo and select Shut Down. You'll be asked to confirm with a dialogue box and will be able to save progress in open apps.

2. To force shutdown, just hold down the power button, although this will mean you'll lose unsaved progress in apps.

> ## Hot Tip
> You can control which apps automatically open on starting your Mac by going to System Preferences > Users & Groups > Login Items and there add or subtract apps.

PUTTING YOUR MAC TO WORK

PUTTING THE APPS IN MAC

Your new computer comes with a host of built-in applications, made by Apple, to enhance your experience. Chapter Two dealt in general terms with apps and how to move between them. Now let's take a look at some of the specifics regarding getting the best from these apps.

WHAT HAVE YOU GOT?

Apple would like us all to think, in one way, shape or form, that it offers all the tools you need to achieve all you need on a Mac. While that's not quite the case, the OS X software is a very good start. There's an email app for sending and receiving correspondence, a web browser for looking

Above: The OS X software may not have everything but it does have a large number of useful apps.

at the Internet, a couple of notepads, a photo locker, a video editor, a messaging portal, a media player, a calendar, an address book, a Maps app and many more little widgets.

What Haven't You Got?

So what do you need to buy? Well, there's no Microsoft Office built-in for a start. That means no Word, no PowerPoint, no Excel and no Outlook, but you can get it. There's no Adobe Photoshop either, there's no Skype, no Google Chrome and no Spotify music player. That's the bad news....

Above: Visit the Mac App store to download apps which did not come with your Mac.

How Do I Get Them?

But now the good news. You can get all of those apps, very, very easily, from the Mac App Store, through the Internet or through other portals. A lot of the ones we mentioned are free, while you'll have to fork out a bit of cash for others.

GOING ON SAFARI

A decade or more ago, Internet connectivity wasn't at the forefront of people's minds when buying a computer. Now, getting online is a primary concern. Your Mac comes with Apple's own Safari web browser and is represented by the compass icon in the dock. Open it up and let's explore.

Hot Tip

Are you connected to the Internet yet? If not, go to System Preferences > Network for help connecting to your home and public network, or see Chapter Five for full details.

The Safari Window

The default opening page in Safari is really quite useful. It shows thumbnails of the websites you visit most often for easy, one-click access, a list of any pages you have bookmarked for future reference and of course the URL bar where you type in your www dots.

Hot Tip

The Top Sites homepage can be accessed at any time by hitting the grid icon in the Favorites Bar, and remember you can go full screen at any time (Command + Shift + F).

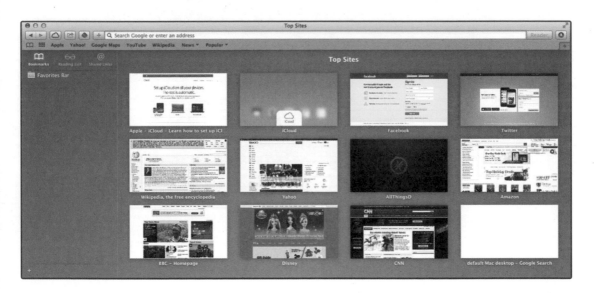

Above: Whenever you start Safari, it will show thumbnails of often-visited websites, for quick access to them.

Opening A Webpage

With the Safari window open, the world (wide web) is your oyster. To open a favourite webpage, let's say bbc.co.uk, place your cursor in the URL bar at the top of the page and click. Then simply type bbc.co.uk on the keyboard and hit the Enter/Return key. A few seconds later (depending on the speed of your Internet connection), you'll see something resembling this....

Above: Type in the name of the website, hit enter and simply wait for it to load. It should only take a few seconds.

Searching The Web

The web holds a wealth of information and Safari, via a search engine of your choosing, will help you find exactly what you need. You can browse to your favourite search engine by going to Google.com, Bing.com or whatever. However, you can simply type your search terms into the URL bar. For example, 'restaurants in London' will load applicable results. To set your default search engine, head to Safari in the menu bar and select Preferences.

Start Your Own Tab(s)

You'll want to keep some pages open while you navigate around the web. This is where tabs come in really handy. They allow you to open multiple pages within the same window and easily switch between them, allowing you to keep Facebook, Twitter and Sky Sports open while you listen to the news on the BBC iPlayer or watch a movie on Netflix.

1. To open a new tab in Safari, simply use the keyboard shortcut Command + T or hit the + icon in the top right corner.

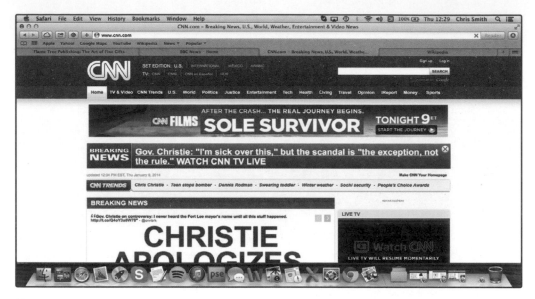

Above: Tabs are a handy way to switch between different webpages withut having multiple windows open.

2. To close an unwanted tab hit Command + W, or hover over the tab and click the x icon.

3. To move between tabs use Control + Tab or just click the individual tabs. Got it? Good.

Hot Tip

The Show All Tabs icon in the top right corner is a neat tool, allowing users to scroll through all open tabs, rather than clicking individual tabs.

Using iCloud Tabs

Are you an iPhone or iPad user running iOS 7? The new Safari brings iCloud tabs into play. This means if you've recently accessed a page on another device associated with your Apple ID, it'll remember that page across your devices, syncing almost instantly via iCloud (see page 48). This is great if you've started reading an article on your iPhone but want to see it on the larger screen when you get home, or vice versa.

1. On your Mac, click the iCloud button in the Safari toolbar to see the open windows on your iOS device.

2. To ensure it's working, go to System Preferences > iCloud and make sure you're signed in and that Safari is ticked.

Reading List

Reading List is perfect if you're at work and spot something you might like to read on your lunch break. To add a webpage to your Reading List, simply hit the plus (+) icon next to the URL bar. Then, to access the Reading List, click the Show Sidebar icon (looks like an open book) in the Favorites bar.

Hot Tip

Just like iCloud tabs, the Reading List also syncs across your other Apple-enabled devices. If you have an iPhone and iCloud enabled, items you've added to your Reading List on your Mac will be available on your mobile phone.

Above: Save webpages to your Reading List for quick access later on. To add a page, click the plus (+) icon next to the URL bar.

Safari Basics

Without going into too much detail, here are a few Safari essentials to help you along the way.

1 **Back/Forward arrows**: Move between pages in a specific tab.

2 **Share icon**: Share the link to a webpage via Mail, Messages, Twitter, Facebook and more. You can also add it to your Bookmarks or Reading List.

3 **Add bookmarks**: Hit the Command + D shortcut to save a page and choose where you want to keep it. Selecting favorites bar from the drop-down menu keeps it in view at all times.

Above: The download icon will show you how long current downloads will take and allow you to open recently downloaded items.

④ **Refresh**: If you want to see the latest version of a webpage (especially if you're following a sports game!) click the curved arrow in the URL bar or use the Command + R keyboard shortcut.

⑤ **Downloads**: Whenever you download a file from the web, be it an email attachment, photo, video or program, you'll see it pop into the download icon in the top right corner. Click this to see recently downloaded files. They can be opened directly from here.

Windows: We've talked about tabs, which we find the best way to work, but if you prefer to work in brand new windows, just use the Command + N shortcut or select File > New Window.

Other Web Browsers

Although Safari is a great browser that comes built into your Mac, it's not the only horse (or zebra?) in the race. Actually, as of recently, it's only taking up about 16 per cent of the market on Mac and PC. Here are some other options.

Above: Google Chrome is particularly good for users of multiple Google services.

○ **Google Chrome**: The world's most popular web browser is available to download at Chrome.com. It's great if you use a lot of Google apps and services like Gmail, YouTube, Google Drive and Google+ as it synchronizes your experience under one login.

○ **Firefox**: Made by Mozilla, this is another popular alternative which is good for plentiful add-ons, widgets and customization.

SPREADING THE MESSAGE

Another absolutely essential function of any computer is the ability to communicate with friends, family and colleagues electronically. The Mail, Messages and FaceTime apps are built-in solutions but there are plenty of other ways to stay in touch using your Mac.

THE MAIL APP

Thanks to email you can send written correspondence, pictures, videos, documents and practically anything else you desire in seconds. Naturally, your Mac has you covered. The most efficient way to manage your email on your Mac is through the built-in Mail app. It's extremely easy to set up, supports multiple accounts, multiple email providers and it also plays nicely with other applications like Safari, Messages, iPhoto and iTunes.

Setting Up Your Email Account

You'll find the Mail app within the dock as it's one of the default apps built into your Mac. It's not difficult to find; it's a stamp. Makes sense, right? Click it and once the icon finishes bouncing, you can start setting up your account.

1. You'll see a Welcome to Mail window, which can be by-passed with a click of the Continue button.

2. Choose your account. If you use a webmail service like Gmail, Exchange Yahoo Mail, or AOL, simply select yours from the list. If you use Microsoft Outlook (previously known as Hotmail) or another provider pick 'Add another account'.

3. On the next screen, enter your full name (this will be what the recipient sees when your email arrives) and then enter the username and password that you use to log into your

email account on the web and select Create. If Apple recognizes the account, you should be good to go and emails will begin flooding in.

4. Having trouble configuring your email? Check out page 244.

THE MAIL WINDOW

The Mail app works off a tabbed interface that makes it easy to move between the following tabs (see image on page 96).

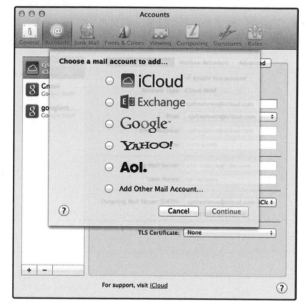

Step 2: Choose the type of mail account you use.

○ **Mailboxes:** Here you'll see all of your associated email accounts as well as sent messages, drafts, junk, trash and other folders.

○ **Messages:** This is a list of the messages you've received in chronological order. Within each box you'll see the name of the sender, the time sent, the amount of messages within the conversation, whether there are attachments, whether you have read or replied to the email and a preview of the email's content. Apple packs a little into a small space here.

○ **Conversation View:** The far right tab displays the most currently selected email, along with the content and the conversation as a whole. You can also view any attachments within this window.

Hot Tip

To add multiple accounts, head to Mail > Preferences in the menu bar. Browse to accounts and hit the + icon. Repeat the process listed above.

⊙ **Toolbar:** There's also a toolbar with access to regularly used commands like New Message, Reply, Reply All, Forward and Delete, while you can also search your mailboxes for content by clicking in the search box and typing names, subjects, content and more.

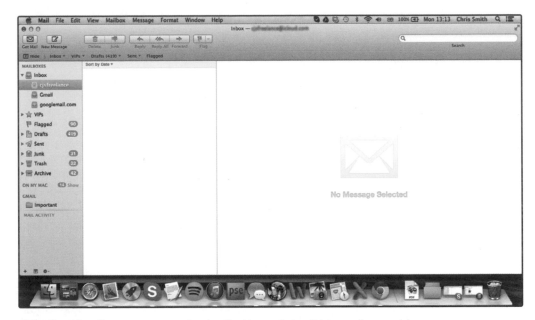

Above: The toolbar offers common commands such as New Message, Reply or Delete, as well as a search box.

Email Basics

Email is all about giving and receiving. To send a brand-new email, hit the pencil and notepad New Message icon in the top left of the Mail window to open a new blank message.

⊙ **To:** Here you'll need to type the email address of your recipient. It'll usually take the form of something like

Hot Tip

If you're having a little trouble getting used to what all of the icons represent within an app, right click on the icon and select Icon and Text. It'll tell you exactly what function a click will perform.

john.johnson@email.com. Regardless of the preface, the @ sign followed by the domain name (@gmail.com, etc.) is essential.

○ If you have your contacts set up either through iCloud, or the Address Book app, you can click the blue + and select from your contacts.

○ In some cases, if contacts are familiar to the app or the Mac, addresses will auto fill as you begin to type the address or their actual name. This will become more effective the more you use the app, as it remembers addresses you've sent to and received from before.

○ **CC**: If you wish to 'copy in' another person, place their email address here. This is usually deployed when an email contains information pertinent to a person, but isn't directly addressed to them.

○ **Subject**: Just a general description of what the email regards will suffice here.

○ **From**: If you have more than one account set up, you'll need to choose which account it is sent from by selecting from the drop-down box here.

Composing Emails

Now that's all of the boring stuff out of the way, you can focus on the content itself, the messages of love, the holiday plans, the funny photographs or the work presentation you're really proud of. Just tap in the empty text box and begin typing. If you're simply sending a text-based email, you can just hit Send and away it goes.

Above: Click the paperclip icon to add attachments to emails.

Hot Tip
To start a new email with an attachment, simply drag the file name, or icon on to the Mail app. Alternatively, right click a file, browse to Share and select Mail.

Adding Attachments

A lot of the time you'll want to add more than just text to your emails. In this case you need to click the paperclip icon in the New Message window. This loads a dialogue box where you can choose which files are to be attached. It looks just like the Finder window, so navigate to your files as you normally would and click Choose File.

Changing The Look And Feel Of Your Emails

In the New Message window you'll see an 'A'. Tapping this opens the text formatting, allowing you to customize fonts, text size, colour, style (bold, italic, underline) and more. Like other apps such as Word, Pages, TextEdit, etc. text must be highlighted before changes are effected. Remember, Command + A selects all text.

Receiving Emails

If you've set up your email address correctly (see page 94), emails should come through as they arrive. This is called 'Push' email. It means you don't have to keep tapping the Get Mail button in the Mail toolbar. When a new message arrives, you'll hear an alert and get a notification in the top right corner. Click this to go straight to the email.

If you miss the notification, the amount of unread emails you've received appears as a number upon the Mail app in the dock. Pretty useful, if you ask us.

Reading Emails

Such is the way the Mail app is configured, you need to do very little to read your emails. Simply choose the Mailbox, select the message from the message list tab and the content will appear in the right-hand tab. If it is part of a conversation, you'll be able to scroll through all of the other emails sent and received.

Hot Tip

An unread email in a conversation thread is represented by a blue dot within the Message tab, next to the sender, subject, date and content preview.

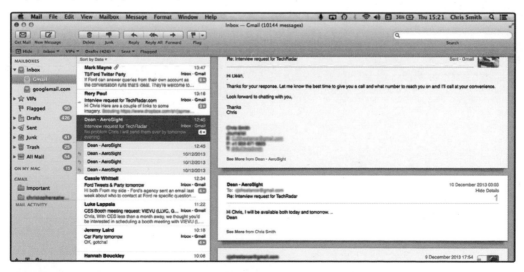

Above: The Mail app allows easy scrolling through messages in the same conversation.

Replying And Forwarding

Within the conversation view on the far right, you have all of the tools you'll need to reply to correspondence. Each of these commands opens the reply in a new window. All you need to do is add your content, further recipients and click send.

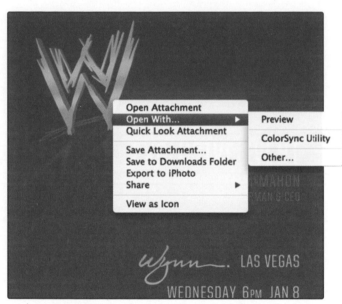

Above: Choose which app you would prefer to open the attachment with, by selecting Open With... from the options.

Opening And Saving Attachments

Attachments will happily sit in your inbox for ever, but you'll often need to act upon them. Right clicking the attachment allows you to do the following.

- ○ **Open**: Opens the app with a default program. For example, photos will always open in Preview.

- ○ **Open With**: Choose the app with which to open. Perhaps you'd rather use iPhoto?

- ○ **Save Attachment**: Choose where you'd like to keep it on your Mac (Desktop, Pictures, Downloads, etc.).

- ○ **Quick Look**: Quickly reveals the contents of the attachment without the need to fully open in an app.

Hot Tip

You can reply to or delete emails directly from the notification alert that appears in the top right corner when an email arrives.

Deleting Emails

Heaven knows, we all get blighted with email spam and junk from time to time, but it can be dispatched immediately. When an email is selected in the Message view, simply hit Delete, or click the trashcan in the toolbar or the conversation view.

MESSAGES

The Messages app is a relatively new addition to Mac OS X and comes over from the mobile world. It allows you to exchange short messages, photos, files and more with anyone using a Mac and also an Apple iPhone, iPad and iPod touch running iOS 5 and higher. It is built into your Mac and is represented by a blue speech bubble in the dock.

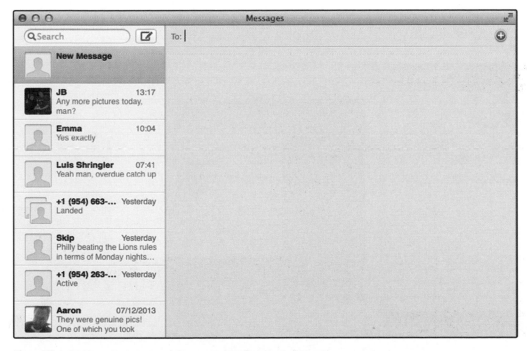

Above: When the Messages app is opened, the message log will automatically appear.

Setting Up Messages

Establishing Messages will be different for different users, but once it's set up you'll never look back.

For those using iOS devices, their phone number and Apple ID (*see page 47*) will already be associated with Messages. Opening the app should immediately bring up your message log. For completely new users, if you set up your Mac with an Apple ID, this will be the default account available when you first open Messages and anything you send will be from the associated email account.

Are you still with us?

Hot Tip

If a number or email address is configured with iMessage it'll appear blue in the 'To' section. Otherwise it'll be red. Send to a red and they won't receive it. Blue, you're all good.

Above: Your messages will appear in a different coloured speech bubble to the person you are talking to.

If you didn't enter your Apple ID when setting up your Mac, open the Messages app, click the title in the menu bar and browse to Preferences > Accounts. There you can sign in with your Apple ID.

Sending Messages

As we mentioned, you can send free messages from your Mac to anyone with an Apple ID. That means you can text people's phones using their actual phone number (providing they have an iPhone) and receive replies on your Mac or any other Apple devices you have. Everything is nicely synced through iCloud.

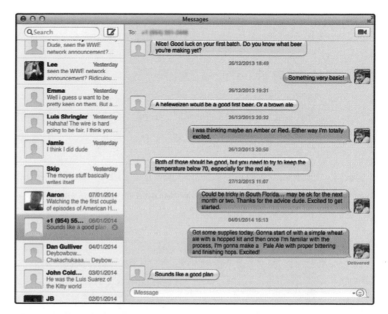

Above: Add pictures to a message by dragging them from a Finder window.

1. To start a new message, hit the pencil and notepad icon in the sidebar and add the iPhone number or Apple ID-associated email address of the person you wish to contact. If your contacts are synced, you can hit the blue + button to find recipients.

2. Then simply type in the text box at the foot of the window and hit enter when you're done. The message will appear above in the conversation view and will be marked with 'Delivered' once it has successfully arrived with the recipient.

3. All future messages between the two parties will appear within this feed as they appear as text messages on smartphones.

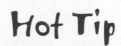

Hot Tip

To send pictures, audio files and short videos, locate the item in Finder, drag it into the conversation window and drop it.

GETTING IN A LITTLE FACETIME

Within the Messages app, you'll see a video camera icon in the top left corner. This is FaceTime. It allows you to make free video calls to other Mac, iPhone, iPod touch or iPad users, as long as the models and software are relatively up to date (iOS 5 or Mac OS X Lion). You'll also find a separate FaceTime app within your Applications folder.

Making FaceTime Calls

If you hit the FaceTime camera app in Messages, it will summon the standalone FaceTime application, activate the Mac's built-in FaceTime camera (MacBooks and iMacs only) and begin dialling the recipient. Until you get an answer you'll see your own appearance in the window.

If the call is answered, you'll sink into the bottom left corner and the recipient will appear. You'll be able to see each other and chat providing your audio is up and your microphone is activated (*see* page 40).

Above: The FaceTime app allows you to make free video calls with other Apple users.

Calling From The FaceTime App

FaceTime has its own standalone app in the Applications folder. Starting a FaceTime conversation is pretty straightforward if you have your Address Book set up (see page 114). From the sidebar, select Contacts and choose from the alphabetical list, select the name and hit FaceTime to commence the call.

Receiving FaceTime Calls

Naturally, you can also receive incoming FaceTime calls. An incoming call will be greeted with an onscreen graphic, the name of the caller and the opportunity to accept or decline.

Left: Once you have accepted an incoming call, you will be able to see the other user and chat to them.

MacBook Air

Alternative Text And Video Chat

While Messages and FaceTime are great free tools, they're rather exclusive. If you have friends on PCs and Android phones you wish to text/video chat with, you'll have to download and install Skype (www.skype.com/mac), or try Google hangouts (google.com/chat/video).

STAYING PRODUCTIVE ON YOUR MAC

As tempting as it is to spend all day browsing the Internet and FaceTiming with friends, we bought a Mac to get some serious work done. In this section we'll introduce you to the available tools.

THE iWORK SUITE

If you're an experienced PC user (or have at least used one), you'll be familiar with Microsoft Office, which features Word, Excel and PowerPoint. iWork is Apple's answer to Microsoft Office and as of late 2013 is free with all new Macs.

What's In iWork?

There are three key apps within iWork. They are Pages, Numbers and Keynote.

- **Pages**: Allows you to create, save and share word-processed documents. As well as those blank documents, you can also fashion attractive flyers and posters, business cards, résumés, letters and more from elegant templates. Compared to Microsoft Word it is quite a simplified, pared-down option.

- **Numbers:** The Apple-made equivalent of Microsoft Excel. This spreadsheet creation tool is capable of so much more. It enables users to create attractive, easy-to-follow charts and reports to brighten up those numbers.

- **Keynote:** Apple's interpretation of Microsoft PowerPoint, it helps you to create good-looking office presentations, which actually stand some chance of capturing your audience's attention.

Inside An iWork App: Pages

As each of these apps could probably demand a chapter in this book, we're just going to take a closer look at Pages here, as all three apps operate on quite similar principles.

To start work within Pages, find it in your Applications folder and open the app. You'll be greeted with the Choose A Template screen. Select Blank Document.

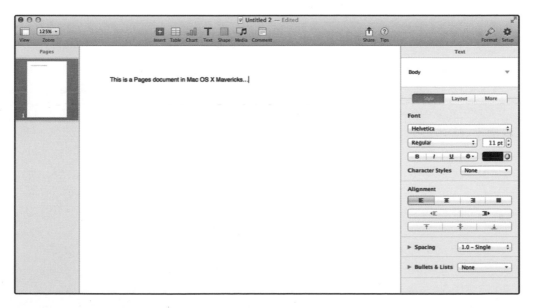

Above: Pages is the document program within iWork. To start a new document, simply select Blank Document and start typing.

Immediately, you can begin typing within the app.

1. To add the Charts, Tables, Shapes and Media (this includes music and video), use the relevant items in the toolbar.

2. To use the Format sidebar to change the look and appearance of text, select the text in question and choose options from the font, size, colour, spacing, style and alignment options.

3. Hit the View section of the toolbar.

4. To save progress, hit Command + S, choose a filename and a destination.

5. To easily share from within the app, hit Share in the toolbar > iCloud and then select Email, Messages, AirDrop (see page 169) and even Facebook and Twitter.

Hot Tip
You can quit iWork apps without saving and not have to worry about losing your work. The app autosaves and re-opens in the last place you left it. We'd still save to be on the safe side though!

Hot Tip
Collaboration is the key for iWork in iCloud. When working within the browser, you can copy the link and share it with fellow iCloud users. Anyone with an Apple ID can now work on the document.

Alternatives To iWork
If you don't have free iWork, the apps can be downloaded from the Mac App Store relatively cheaply. However, there are ways to access productivity apps without forking out more money. Notes (see page 113) and TextEdit are built in apps that allow you to get down your thoughts. However, there's also iWork for iCloud.

iWork In iCloud
Another 2013 addition, iWork in iCloud allows everyone with an Apple ID to use web-based versions of Pages, Numbers and Keynotes and save them in the iCloud. Head to iCloud.com and sign in using your Apple ID and you'll see access to those apps on your homepage.

Hot Tip

Rather than buying iWork apps, you may wish to consider Microsoft Office for Mac. Go to Office.com/Mac for information on how to download the old faithful.

Above: If you prefer Microsoft Office, you can download this for your Mac.

If you have iWork on your computer, then iWork in iCloud becomes a more important tool. The latest versions of all of your documents will be synced across all of your devices automatically and stored safely in the iCloud. If you've been working on a spreadsheet on your Mac and switch computers, you can pick up where you left off by logging into iCloud, even if you're using a Windows PC.

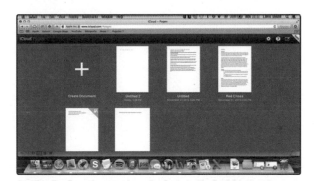

Above: iCloud syncs your iWork documents across all your devices.

Saving To And Opening From iCloud

You can automatically save a document, spreadsheet or presentation to iCloud by hitting Save and selecting iCloud as a destination. All documents saved in iCloud can be opened by selecting Open from the menu and selecting iCloud. These will be the most recent versions.

Above: Open documents saved to iCloud for the most recent version.

ORGANIZING YOUR LIFE

Your Mac is a great tool for work and play, but knowing that you may need a little help co-ordinating your hectic lifestyle, Mac OS X also features a host of tools to help you stay on top of where you need to be and what you need to be doing.

CALENDAR

The Mac OS X calendar is a very underrated feature. It's a massively helpful tool that works across apps, devices, accounts, social networks and syncs everything automatically. Open it up from the dock and your Applications folder.

Above: Events in the Calendar window are colour coded according to where the information is sourced from.

The Calendar Window

When you open the Calendar, you can choose to view the day, week, month or year. Events from different calendar accounts and Facebook events are colour-coded. Clicking them will reveal more information about said event.

Adding An Event

The quickest way to schedule an event in the Calendar app is simply to press the plus button in the window and type in what you're doing. For example, 'Coffee with Karen at 7pm on Friday'. This will immediately add it to the calendar.

Above: To add an event, press the plus button and type in the details.

Adding Accounts To Your Calendar

It is likely that any Internet accounts (check within System Preferences) you've already set up, such as your Apple ID, Facebook and email accounts, are also pulling information into the Calendar. You can add others by heading to Calendar > Preferences > Accounts and following the same procedure outlined on page 94 in the Mail section.

Syncing Calendars

Once you've set up your Calendar, you can take comfort in the knowledge that all events will be synced back to that account across all devices. So, if you add an event to your iCloud calendar it'll appear on your Mac, iPhone, iPad and at iCloud.com. Likewise an event set up on your iPhone will be synced back to your Mac. If you add an event to your Gmail calendar from your Mac, it'll show up in your Google Calendar on the web. Thanks iCloud, you're a real pal.

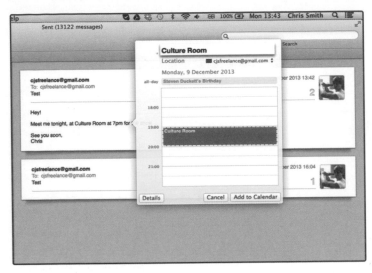

Above: You can click a time or date in an email message to add the event to the Calendar app.

Calendar/Mail Integration

The Calendar app plays really nicely with the Mail app: if someone sends you an email saying, for example, let's meet at 1pm on Thursday, you can click this text to add a Calendar event for that time, for which you'll then receive a reminder. This also works for other dates and times that appear within emails, such as travel arrangements and ticket purchase confirmation emails.

Sending Invites

As well as receiving invites through Mail, you can also send them on. Just set up an event in the Calendar. Double click it and begin typing invitees. You can add a full email address and existing contacts will be auto filled in. Send the invite. Once it has been accepted or declined, you'll receive an email.

Calendar Alerts

A digital calendar wouldn't be much use if it didn't give you fair warning of what's coming up. You can head to Calendar > Preferences > Alerts to configure when you get these alerts and how they appear. They also appear in the Notifications Center (see page 115), allowing you to view events at any time, without heading to the Calendar app.

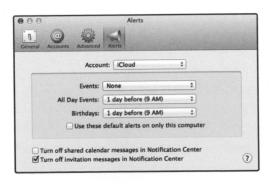

Above: Set up alerts to remind you of calendar events.

REMINDERS, CONTACTS, NOTES, STICKIES, DASHBOARD

While the Calendar app will alert you to appointments, for the basic day-to-day Honeydos (you know, 'honey do this, honey do that') the Reminders app comes in very handy.

Above: Use Reminders for day-to-day things.

Setting Reminders And Ticking Them Off

Reminders is another of those apps that, thanks to iCloud, plays nicely with iOS devices and iCloud.com, so you can set reminders on your Mac and then go around ticking them off on your iPhone (if you have one) or other computer. To set Reminders, open the app from your Applications folder.

1. In the Today pane, hit the + icon and begin typing. Once you've written the text press + again to add further items.

2. To set Reminders for the future, hit the Calendar icon in the app, select the date and then repeat the step above.

3. To tick off items, tick the box to the left of the text, to push them into the Completed section.

Hot Tip

To ensure items are being synced across Mac OS X and iOS devices, make sure you're adding Reminders under the iCloud pane rather than On My Mac. The latter just works locally.

Notes

The Notes app is different to TextEdit and Pages as it's more for your random musings and thoughts than anything else. Here you can jot down anything you wish, add pictures and other attachments and they'll be

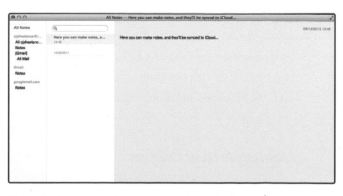

Above: The Notes app is perfect for random musings and collecting pictures.

stored on your Mac. If you add Notes to your iCloud preferences, they'll also be synced to your other devices and available at iCloud.com.

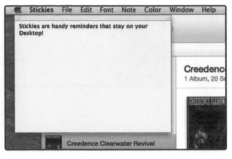

Above: Stickies are like virtual sticky notes.

To add to Notes, open the app, hit the + to create a new note and simply begin typing. Everything is saved and synced automatically.

Stickies

Are you the type to leave sticky notes all over your desk at work? Then you'll love the Mac equivalent: Stickies. It's like Notes, but sits nicely on your desktop as a constant reminder of a phone number, activity or email address.

YOUR CONTACTS BOOK

It may be that you seldom open the Address Book app on your Mac, but the presence of those contacts underpins other apps like Mail, Messages, Calendar and more.

Importing Contacts

You can add contacts manually. That's cool. However, your other Internet accounts are probably loaded with information. In System Preferences > Internet Accounts, browse through your accounts and check the Contacts tick box to pull everything in. This will bring in Google, Microsoft, Facebook, Twitter accounts and more, plus any contacts you've synced to iCloud.

Above: Add the details for a new contact.

Adding A New Contact

If you'd like to manually add a new contact, open the app and use the keyboard shortcut Command + N to load a blank card. Type in their vital statistics using the tab key to move between fields.

Acting Upon Contacts

To interact with a contact, tap the indicator next to their phone number/email address and select from the actions. You can email, call through Skype or FaceTime, send messages and more.

NOTIFICATIONS CENTER AND ALERTS

The Notifications Center is another relatively new addition to Mac OS X. It's one of those useful features that you forget is there. You can access it by tapping the list icon in the top right corner of the menu bar.

What's In The Notifications Center?

Anything that sends you updates, events or messages; your recent emails, Facebook notifications, Twitter mentions, available App Store updates, Skype messages, Calendar events and so on. You can configure exactly what you'll be notified about, and how you'll be notified by heading to System Preferences > Notifications.

Above: The Notification Center contains messages and updates from your apps.

Above: Change how your alerts appear.

Alerts

Also within System Preferences > Notifications, you can configure how the alerts appear within the top right corner for each and every app. For example, if you select Mail, you can choose to have no alert, you can choose a banner, which will fade after a couple of seconds, or an alert that requires your attention before it goes away. Other options include showing notifications on the lock screen, showing message previews and playing a sound along with the notification. Play around and see what works for you.

FINDING YOUR WAY AROUND IN MAPS

In 2013, Apple introduced its fledgling Maps app into the OS X fold and it sure does look pretty. It's also great for finding directions to friends' houses, meetings, restaurants and everything in between.

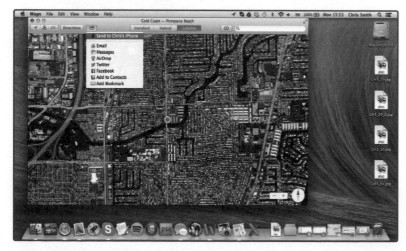

Above: The Maps app makes it easy to share your location.

The View From Up High

There are three ways to view Maps in the Mavericks app: Standard shows a Map interface complete with markings; Satellite shows the real deal from those little gadgets in orbit; and Hybrid is a mixture of the two. You'll see these options in the centre of the toolbar.

Where Am I?

You can navigate directly to your current location by hitting the compass arrow in the top left corner.

Getting Directions With Your Mac

The primary purpose of this app is to assist users in finding their way from A to B. Maps will provide you with detailed turn-by-turn route information, which you can share with other people, print off, or even send directly to the Maps app on your iPhone before you set off. Here's how to get those directions.

Step 3: Enter start and end locations, then press Enter to load directions.

1. Hit the Search bar in the top right of the window and type in the name or address of your destination. When it appears in the drop-down options, click it.

2. Hit Directions in the toolbar to load the address as your end point.

3. Type in the name and address of your starting point (if your address is configured with your Mac or Apple ID somehow, you can just type Home) and hit enter to load directions.

4. Use the indicators to toggle between walking and driving directions.

Sharing Locations And Directions

Within Maps it's possible to share your location or directions through Mail, Messages, Twitter, Facebook and more. This feature is really helpful in a number of ways.

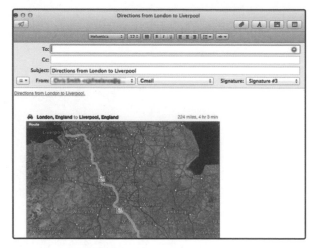

Above: You can send the directions in an email for others to print and use.

- **Share a location on social media:** To let people know where an event is taking place.

- **Share directions via email and messages:** Plot a route for friends and family to follow that they can print off on their journey.

- **Email to yourself:** Print off the PDF and use it on the road.

- **Send to iOS:** A great feature that allows you to send the directions you've just plotted to another device where they can be followed along the journey with voice-powered turn-by-turn navigation assistance.

- **Add to Contacts:** If you have a friend's address up, you can select this and attach the address to their phone number and other details.

Points Of Interest

Maps is also useful for finding places to visit in your local area. Simply click on a place of interest to get contact information and even reviews from Yelp.com.

Hot Tip

In selected cities you can use the Flyover tool, which allows you to tour famous cities from the comfort of your office chair. Where Flyover is available you can zoom in and hit the 3D icon in the toolbar. Then use multi-touch gestures (two fingers on the trackpad to pan, pinch to zoom) to navigate the skyline.

WHAT'S ON YOUR DASHBOARD?

We've mentioned the Mac dashboard a couple of times but haven't delved in yet. The dashboard is filled with useful widgets like a mini calendar, a calculator, a weather forecast, currency converter and more. It's perfect for times when you don't need a full application.

Above: The dashboard contains a multitude of useful widgets.

How To Access It

Where is this mysterious dashboard then? Well, it has its own area of the OS away from everything else. You can select Mission Control (see page 77) and then choose dashboard, or you can access it through a multi-touch gesture. We use a left swipe with four fingers to move to the dashboard. This can be configured in trackpad preferences.

Customizing To The Dashboard

On your dashboard you'll see the widgets mentioned above, but you can add more by clicking the + icon and delete others using the – button. You can add flight trackers, world clocks, local cinema screenings and more.

Hot Tip

You can easily move widgets around the dashboard by picking them up and dragging them to a new destination.

Above: Customize the dashboard by adding other widgets.

SHOWING YOUR SOCIAL SIDE

Love it or loathe it, the social-networking era isn't going anywhere and your Mac is teeming with tools to allow you to get the most from Facebook, Twitter and the rest. Sometimes you'll need to go on the web, but there are also some neat built-in tools.

BUILT-IN ACCESS

In the newest version of Mac OS X, access to Twitter and Facebook is built-in at 'OS level', meaning your Mac will check Twitter and Facebook for you and deliver any notifications to your desktop, without having to visit Twitter.com or Facebook.com. It'll also sync with other apps on your Mac and enable you to share content directly to these services.

Adding Internet Accounts

If you browse to System Preferences > Internet Accounts you'll see the email addresses and iCloud accounts you already have configured with your Mac. From here, it's easy to add more accounts from some of the web's most popular services. Even though the configuration of accounts registered to Twitter, Facebook, LinkedIn, Flickr and so on differ, let's use Facebook as an example.

Configuring Facebook On Your Mac

Head to Internet Accounts within System Preferences, Click the + button and select Facebook and enter your username and password. If it is accepted you'll see a screen informing you that Facebook is syncing your friends' contact details to the Address Book

Hot Tip

If you wish to remove Facebook's influence over your Address Book and Calendar, go to System Preferences > Internet Accounts, select Facebook and untick those boxes.

app and bringing birthdays
and event notifications into
the Calendar app.

It also enables you to share
photos directly to Facebook
from Finder, Safari, Mail,
Messages, iPhoto and more.
Finally, logging in through
Facebook allows compatible
Mac Store Apps to play
nicely with your account.

Facebook Notifications On Your Mac

One of the key benefits
of configuring your Mac

Above: Configure Facebook on your Mac in order to sync contact and event
information, as well as making it easier to share files from your Mac with Facebook.

with a social-network or Internet account is the notifications. In terms of Facebook, if you
receive a tag, comment, message or virtually anything else, you'll see a notification pop up in
the top right corner of the screen. Clicking these alerts will take you straight to Facebook.com
on the web (login required).

Knowing the notifications are coming through in real-time means you're less likely to waste
time checking Facebook in case someone commented on your photo!

Posting To Facebook (And Twitter) From Your Mac

Usually you have to go to the Facebook.com or Twitter.com websites to post a status,
but if your Mac is set up with your account, you can do it directly from the Notifications
Center (see page 115).

1. Click the Notification icon in the very top right corner of the Menu bar and select Facebook or Twitter.

2. Fill in the card with your Status Update or Tweet and click post.

Posting Photos And Videos To Social Networks

Once your accounts are configured, you can share your pics and short videos from practically anywhere on your Mac. All you need to do is right click (two finger click on trackpad) on a file or icon, cycle through the options and hover over Share. There you'll be able to select the destination. Alternatively, in apps like Preview there's a built-in Share button for open files.

With Facebook this sharing works particularly well. The photo or video opens up in a new card. You can choose the album you'd like to pick, who will see it and add a message too.

Above: Right click on the file you wish to share, select Share, then choose the destination, such as Facebook.

IMPORTING AND WORKING WITH YOUR PHOTOS

Before you go sharing photographs and videos, you've got to get them on to your Mac. Thankfully it's really simple to import media from your camera and keep those special memories safe.

iPHOTO

Many apps are given the iSomething moniker and so it should come as no surprise that iPhoto looks after your precious photos. It comes built into all Macs and is represented by the camera/photo icon in the dock.

Importing Your Pictures

There's nothing worse than losing/breaking a memory card packed with holiday snaps that can never be replaced, so it's important that you import photos at the earliest opportunity. iPhoto makes it easy.

1. Once you plug in your digital camera or mobile device, either via the USB cable or by removing the memory card and plugging it into your Mac (either with a memory card adapter or through the built-in SD card slot), iPhoto should begin bouncing in the dock and open.

2. Immediately, you'll see all photos on the card/camera load on to an import screen within the app. The camera will appear under Devices in the sidebar within iPhoto.

3. Select each of the photos you wish to import (remember what we said about batch selecting items on page 65) and hit Import Selected. Alternatively, you can just import everything.

Step 5: Once you have imported the selected photos, they will remain on your Mac's hard drive.

4. Once the upload is complete, iPhoto will ask if you want to keep or delete the imported photos from your memory card. Unless your card is filling up, keep them for now.

5. Next you'll be taken straight to the Import page, and your photos now reside on your Mac's hard drive.

6. Browse to Events in the Library section, scroll to the newest batch, click the title and type in a name.

Other Import Options

If you have photos on your phone or perhaps some lying around your computer and you want to bring them into the iPhoto fold, it's pretty straightforward. Select File > Import to Library (Command + Shift + I) and browse to the files of your choosing within the pop-up dialogue box.

Browsing With iPhoto

There's so much you can do within iPhoto. Double click any of the thumbnail photos and it will fill the window. Here you can do the following.

○ **Give it a name!**: Usually, the file name will sit here, but tap it and add your own.

○ **Add a description**: See above.

○ **Rate it**: Tap the stars to signal how good this photo is. Great if you're planning to create albums.

○ **Zoom**: Want a closer look at a certain aspect of the photo? Use the zoom scroller in the left corner of the iPhoto window. You'll see a little Navigation tab pop up, which lets you know where you are in the photo.

○ **Edit it**: Click Edit at the bottom right corner of the window to load the options. There are loads of Quick Fixes to get rid of red-eye, crop unwanted elements, rotate, straighten and more. You can also click Effects to add filters like Sepia, or Black and White. The Adjust tab lets you get into some more advanced colour level editing.

Hot Tip

If you're unhappy with any of the changes you've made to your photos, you can hit Undo or Revert to Original within the Edit sidebar at any time.

Working With iPhoto

Lets say, just for argument's sake, that all of your snaps are now sitting comfortably within iPhoto, perfectly organized into events and albums. (Hey! We can dream, can't we?) What else can we do?

○ **Merge Events**: Drag and drop one Event on to another.

○ **Faces**: Select the Faces tab in the sidebar to see pictures of individuals within your albums.

Select Find Faces to add more and soon, iPhoto will begin to recognise familiar faces and suggest tags.

○ **Places**: Mobile photos are sometimes geo-tagged, allowing you to hit Places to view where they were taken on a map.

○ **Search**: In the bottom left corner, tap search and type in names, keywords, locations, event names and more.

Sharing From iPhoto

One good thing about using iPhoto to store all of your digital camera and mobile photos all in one place is the one-stop-shop sharing options it provides. If you so desire, you can share single photos or entire albums directly to Facebook. Other options include Mail, Messages, Twitter, Flickr and iCloud. Hit the Share button in the bottom right corner and follow the on-screen instructions.

Be careful not to email too many photos at a time, as most providers have an attachment limit. Gmail for example is 25 MB, which is about 10 hi-res photos.

Hot Tip

Once you've synced your Mac with Facebook (*see* page 120), iPhoto will pull in all of the photos you've uploaded to the site, allowing you to view them within the app.

CREATING PHOTO ALBUMS

Importing new photos will automatically create date-based Events within iPhoto. You may also wish to create custom albums bringing memories together. This is super simple.

1. First select an Event in the sidebar: hit Command + N and a new 'untitled album' will appear beneath Albums in the sidebar featuring all of those photos. Type in a name of your choice.

Above: Sort your photos into different albums. Create new albums and give them names.

2.   To create a brand new empty album, select Photos from the sidebar and hit Command + N. Give it a name.

3.   To add photos to a new or existing album, select the pictures of your choice and drag and drop them on to the album name. Alternatively, select the photos and hit Add To in the bottom right and choose the album.

CREATING iPHOTO BOOKS

iPhoto is great for fashioning custom photo books, calendars or cards that can be delivered straight to your door. You don't even have to upload photos to a website. Providing you're connected, Apple will handle that.

1.   Firstly, gather all of the photos you wish to include in a single album (see above). Click on the album in the sidebar and then click Add To.

2. Here you can choose a photo Book, Calendar or Card. Make a selection and iPhoto will immediately load presentation options.

3. Pick a theme by cycling through the carousel of options presented on the screen. Here you'll also see pricing options and how much each additional page will set you back. You can also select hardcover, soft cover, wired, etc.

4. Once the preview has been fully created you can edit individual pages, add effects to photos, retouch and reframe photos, add captions, rearrange photos and more. There's not enough space to go into it here, but with the tips you've picked up so far, we're confident you can handle it.

5. When you're happy, click Buy Book to enter payment information and before you know it, your creation will be winging its way to you.

Step 3: Cycle through the different presentation options for your photo book.

PHOTOSTREAMS AND iCLOUD

We're afraid this is one of those points where this book only becomes useful for those who are into Apple beyond their Mac computer. If you're an iPhone owner (please don't take photos on your iPad – it looks very silly), iCloud will safeguard photos taken on your phone, automatically uploading up to 1,000 of them to your PhotoStream. iPhoto will download them from the cloud and place them in monthly albums so they can hang out on your computer. Here they can be browsed, edited and shared or simply remain for safekeeping.

To ensure iPhoto is configured with iCloud, go to Internet Accounts, select iCloud and tick the Photos option.

Hot Tip

To send all new photos taken on your camera directly to your iCloud PhotoStream, select iPhoto in the menu bar, click Preferences > iCloud and tick the relevant box.

Above: Photos taken on an iPhone will be automatically uploaded to your PhotoStream via iCloud.

OTHER PHOTO TOOLS

iPhoto is the best way to mange your library on your Mac, but there are loads of other tools that allow you to view and even take photos quickly and easily. There are also tons of additional software you can download.

Quick Look

The quickest way to see a photo that's saved to your Mac is the aptly named Quick Look tool. Right click on an image file and select Quick Look to instantly see the photo. It's great for identifying small thumbnails without opening the image. From here you can close (Command + W), share elsewhere (see page 126) or open in Preview.

Above: Most images will automatically open in Preview, for a quick look.

Preview

The Preview app is the bridge between Quick Look and iPhoto. Double click most images and they'll open in Preview by default. You can zoom, rotate, annotate, share and save elsewhere, but not a lot else. It also opens PDFs and other documents.

Photo Booth

If you want to take self-portraits on your Mac and add fun effects you can use Photo Booth. Open the app from Utilities and create a Photo Booth Library. Your iSight camera will kick in and you can hit the red capture button to take a picture. You can choose to take four photos at once, or record video messages you can share. Hit effects to browse through a host of zany options to distort, contort and discolour your features. Photo Booth is also the default app loaded when you're choosing a new profile picture for your Mac.

Above: Add fun effects to photos with Photo Booth.

INSTALLING NEW APPS

By now you should have a pretty good grasp of what your Mac is capable of out of the box, but there's so much more to enjoy. In this section we'll guide you through finding additional apps, downloading and installing them.

FINDING NEW APPS

There are loads of apps you may have used on your PC that you'd like to bring into the fold on your Mac. Usually that's not a problem, as there are very few apps that don't have a Mac-based version these days. If you head to page 252, you'll find hundreds of 'em. Primarily you'll obtain these apps by two means – either the Mac App Store or by downloading them via the Internet.

Hot Tip
The Mac App Store doesn't have everything, but when downloading from here you'll know that the software has been approved and tested by Apple.

THE MAC APP STORE

Following the success of the iOS App Store, Apple decided to introduce one for the Mac. Previously software was mostly downloaded through the browser or through physical media like pocket hard drives and CDs. In the digital age, you can have the software up and running on your Mac in minutes.

Above: Visit the Mac App store to download new software.

Using The Mac App Store

To open the Store click the 'A' icon in the dock or select the Apple logo in the menu bar and select App Store. Here you'll be able to browse between Featured (apps Apple is promoting), Charts, Categories (Games, Productivity, Music, Business, News, etc.), Purchases (stuff you've downloaded before) and Updates (which offers new versions of apps you've already purchased).

Searching For Apps

If you don't have a specific app in mind, but are looking for something to fulfil a specific need, let's say a Twitter client for your Mac, the easiest way is to Select Categories > Social Networking. This will show you a list of available apps, but also, on the right side of the window you'll see the Top Free and Top Paid apps, keying you into what's popular with other users.

Hot Tip
Keep your eye on the Featured tab, as it offers a good selection of brand-new apps and games as well as Editor's Choices and specially grouped collections like Big Name Games.

Above: The Mac App Store promotes and suggests certain apps to help you find something worth downloading.

If you know what you want, simply type the name into the Search bar. If that app is available within the store, it will come up in the search results. If not, see the section on downloading apps from the Internet (page 134).

Downloading From The Mac App Store

Once you've found the app, hit the Free/Price icon underneath the logo and then Buy App. You'll need to enter your Apple ID password to sign in. If you still haven't created an Apple ID (come on, you really should have by now!), you can do so here. Once you've signed in, the download will begin. You'll see the progress in the Launchpad icon within the dock.

Installing Apps From The Mac App Store

This part is going to be short and sweet. One of the advantages of downloading from the App Store is all of the installation stuff is handled for you. Once a download is complete, head to the app in Launchpad. It'll be surrounded by sparkles! Click to open. You may have to agree to some Ts & Cs, but that's it. You're ready to start using it.

Above: Update alerts will notify you when a new update is available to download.

Updating Apps

Another advantage (they're starting to rack up aren't they?) is the App Store notification when a new version of the app is available to download. You can see Updates within the App Store itself, but you'll also get an alert as soon as an update is available. Clicking this alert opens the App Store, allowing you to update to new versions of apps.

FINDING APPLICATIONS ONLINE

There are loads and loads of popular apps that play perfectly nicely with your Mac but don't feature on the Mac App Store. Apps we've mentioned in this chapter, in fact. Microsoft Word isn't there, Skype isn't there, Google Chrome isn't there and Firefox isn't there. You'll need to go online to get them.

1. Open your Internet browser and type the name of the program into the search bar; for example, 'Skype for Mac'.

2. From the search results, pick the top couple of results as they'll be the most official portals and it'll likely take you straight to where you need to be.

3. Follow the on-screen instructions (you may have to enter details and spend some money before you download) to begin the download.

4. Depending on which browser you use, the download take place in different areas. In Safari, it's to the right of the URL bar. The progress will be depicted by the blue progress bar.

5. Once the download is complete, double click the file from within the Downloads list in Safari.

6. The install file (usually with a .dmg suffix) will begin to unpack and you'll see the app in Finder.

7. Usually, you'll be asked to drag the icon into the Applications folder.

8. Browse to the Applications folder and double click as you usually would. The first time you open you'll be asked whether you trust the web program. Hit open and you're good to go.

Step 7: Drag the icon into the Applications folder when indicated on screen.

ENTERTAINMENT

iTUNES

An application so famous, influential and functional it could fill a book all by itself, iTunes houses your music, movies, TV shows, podcasts, audiobooks and enables you to play them back. It also allows you to purchase content from a vast digital library.

iTUNES MUSIC AND VIDEO

iTunes started off as a music portal (hence the name). Like iPhoto it's a great media library, allowing music to be accessed and played back quickly and easily. Later, we'll talk about buying music and video and streaming music over the Internet, but for now let's focus on playback.

Above: iTunes can be opened by clicking the blue musical note icon on the dock.

Above: There are a number of ways to import music into your iTunes music library.

Getting Your Files On To iTunes

Open up iTunes by clicking the blue musical note in the dock. What do you see? An empty library. To change this you'll need to get your music on to your Mac. There are a number of ways to do this.

○ **Import from hard drive:** If you already have a digital music collection from another PC, then it's easy to bring it into iTunes, providing you've transferred it to a hard drive that can be plugged into your Mac (see page 33). Browse to the files or folders you wish to import, drag them and drop them on the iTunes logo or within the app itself. Alternatively, hit Command + O in iTunes to find them.

○ **Import from CD:** If your Mac has a disc drive or you have an external accessory, you can import your entire CD collection. Music CDs automatically open in iTunes. Simply click Import and the entire CD will be added to your digital library.

○ **Download from iCloud:** If you've purchased music and video from iTunes before using your Apple ID on another computer or mobile device, it can be downloaded freely on to your Mac (see page 146).

iTunes Playback

Now you've actually got some music and videos to play. Hooray. From here it's all pretty smooth sailing in terms of playback. Just double click a song to get started. Let's take a quick look at the iTunes control system.

○ **Play/Pause**: Well, this one, you know, plays and pauses stuff. Space bar for pausing and playing also works pretty well here, as do the keyboard's media controls.

Above: Click the skip arrows to move to the next or previous file.

Above: The progress bar shows how much time is left.

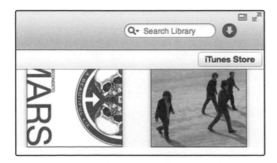

Above: Type in a particular term to search the library.

○ **Skip arrows**: Tap these to move to the next file, hold them to scan backwards and forwards.

○ **Volume**: Drag the scroll bar back and forth.

○ **AirPlay**: Providing another AirPlay device is on the same Wi-Fi network, you can send the content to speakers, or another display (*see* page 140).

○ **Album artwork**: Load the mini-player.

○ **Shuffle**: Play items in a random order.

○ **Now playing**: Click the arrow to load options like add to playlist, go to artist.

○ **Progress bar**: Shows how long has passed and how long is left. Can be clicked or dragged to different sections.

○ **Repeat**: Press once to repeat an album/playlist, twice to repeat the current item.

- **List**: Shows the songs coming up next. Can be selected from the list.

- **Search**: Search library. Click within the field and begin typing.

- **Mini player**: Simplified playback controls.

- **Full screen**: Take your iTunes experience to the max.

Above: The Library drop-down menu allows you to switch between types of media.

- **Library**: Switch between the music, TV shows and movies you have stored on your computer. Each type of media offers different options. For example, Music allows you to switch between songs, albums, artists and more.

- **Devices**: If an iPhone, iPod or iPad is connected via a USB cable or over Wi-Fi, it will appear on the right side next to ...

- **iTunes Store**: Here you can buy music, movies, TV shows, and so much more.

Hot Tip

Want to control your music while doing other things on your computer? Hit 'switch to mini player' to bring up a simple playback controls option. Go to iTunes > Preferences > Advanced to keep the window in front of other apps.

Creating Playlists

The days of the romantic mix tape may be far behind us, but that doesn't mean you can't make killer compilations within your digital music library. The easiest way to do so is to simply hit Command + N (which as you should know by now is the default command for 'New' across the Mac). This will load a playlist in a sidebar on the right.

1. Give it a name by overtyping Playlist 1.

2. Browse to an item you wish to add to the playlist.

3. Select it, drag it and drop it into the sidebar.

4. Repeat until all of the songs/albums/artists you want are on your playlist.

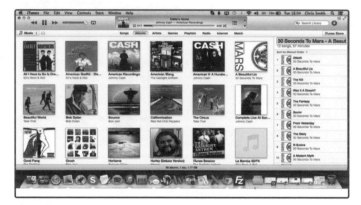

Above: New playlists will appear in a sidebar to the right of the screen.

5. Hit Done.

6. Browse to Playlists in the Library menu bar.

Hot Tip

For a more traditional iTunes app view, select View > Show Sidebar. This can make navigation a little simpler.

iTunes Radio (Coming To UK Soon)

Free music streaming has emerged as an important trend thanks to apps like Spotify that allow users to listen to songs over the Internet without actually buying them. Apple's own version, iTunes Radio, allows users to create and customize radio stations based on a genre, artist or song. The idea is the station will give you more of the same from related artists. Here's how to start a station.

1. Select the Music library in iTunes and browse to Radio in the app's menu bar.

2. You'll see Featured Stations at the top. These are pre-selected stations from Apple or Guest DJs. Double click on an icon to start playing.

Above: Featured stations selected by Apple will appear at the top of the page.

3. To create a station, hit the + icon next to My Stations.

4. Type in the name of a song, artist or genre and allow the field to populate. Click to select your choice.

Hot Tip

Click the song title in iTunes to refine the station's playlist by selecting Play More Like This or Never Play This Song. You can also add songs to your iTunes wish list if you'd like to play the song on command.

Above: You can access Internet radio stations.

iTunes Radio works just like iTunes in terms of controlling the playback, but you'll only get six skips every hour and you'll need to listen to an audio advert every once in a while.

Internet Radio

It's an under-appreciated feature, but iTunes also gives access to hundreds upon hundreds of radio stations across the Internet. Simply select Internet from the Music menu and take your pick to tune into live broadcasts.

THE iTUNES STORE

You thought the free software and free custom radio stations were out of the kindness of Apple's heart? No! They just want you to splash the cash. It's perfectly possible to use iTunes without spending a penny, but with so much choice....

WHAT'S IN THE iTUNES STORE?

This is your one-stop shop for digital media. It's HMV and Blockbuster sitting right within your computer and everything is available to you right now. Whether you want to buy albums and singles, rent or buy films, or buy digital books, everything is here.

Above: Singles, albums, movies, TV shows and books are all available from the iTunes Store.

iTUNES STORE HOMEPAGE

From your library, hit the iTunes Store button on the far right of the window to enter the store. The storefront is a little bit of an assault on the senses. You'll see featured content in a carousel, New Music, New Movies, TV Shows and more. On the right side of the window you'll see the charts for singles, albums, movies, TV shows, apps and books; below quick links for your account details, wish list and more.

Finding What You Want

If you see something that tickles your fancy on the homepage, click it, hit Buy, enter your Apple ID, username and password, and agree to purchase. Otherwise, type your desired album, movie or TV show into the search bar.

Downloading

Any purchases you make on the iTunes Store are yours to keep for ever. As soon as you hit that Buy

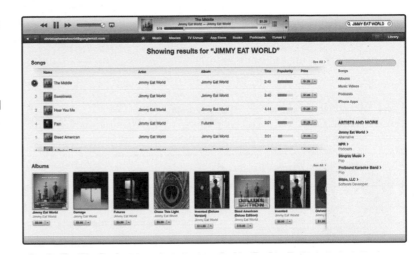

Above: You can search for a particular artist to see a list of all their available songs.

Above: Your Internet connection will determine how quickly items download.

Hot Tip

When renting or buying movies, you can start watching the film while the rest of it downloads. How long the download takes will depend on your Internet connection.

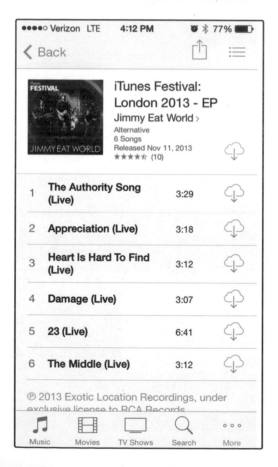

button, the download will start. You can keep track of it in the Now Playing pane, and as soon as individual items finish downloading, they'll be available in your library.

Using iCloud To Reinstate Purchases

Another way to get music/video you own on to your Mac is to re-download stuff you've already purchased from iTunes. It's easy to do through the iTunes Store. On the storefront, hit Purchased and then the iCloud icon next to the purchase items to add them to your Mac library.

Renting Or Buying?

Most things on the iTunes Store are yours to keep and can be transported and re-downloaded to multiple devices until the end of time. This is the case for TV shows, music videos, albums, singles, books, apps and whatever else. However, there is also an option to rent movies.

While it's not available for all movies, on some films (especially new releases) you can select the option to rent for much less than it costs to buy. This will allow you to watch the movie any time in the next 30 days. Once you start watching, you have 24 hours to finish the movie. In that 24 hours you can watch it as many times as you like, but once it expires it will disappear from your hard drive.

Left: It is possible to re-download already purchased items.

YOU GOT GAME

Mac computers have never really been regarded highly as gaming devices, but that doesn't mean you can't enjoy some new and classic titles on your computer. Here's how to get gaming.

GAMES ON THE MAC APP STORE

Enter the App Store (see page 131) and go to Games. There you'll find everything from fun, free time-killers to versions of console and PC classics. It's not as well stocked as the iOS App Store, but there's still plenty to keep you entertained.

Downloading Games From The Mac App Store

Nothing really new to see here. You can download and buy games in the same way you do apps from the Mac App Store. There are Featured Games, Top Charts and so on to be found within the store. You can obtain everything from the Call Of Duty games to simple smartphone stuff like Angry Birds.

Controlling Games On Your Mac

All games downloaded through the Mac App Store can be controlled using your mouse/trackpad and keyboard. You can also connect your Mac to a USB or Bluetooth control pad.

Above: The App Store offers a multitude of games to download.

Game Center

Game Center is a feature borrowed from the iPhone and iPad, like so many others within Mac OS X these days. It allows users to keep track of their gaming achievements, and challenge friends online. It's still a fledgling feature on Mac OS X, but worth checking out.

READING BOOKS

Did you know you can now read books on your Mac, with millions of titles available to purchase from iTunes and the new iBooks app, and what's more all can be synced across your Apple mobile devices?

Above: Access a large library from the iBooks app.

THE iBOOKS APP

This newly introduced app operates in a very similar way to the iTunes Store and the Mac App Store. It gives access to a huge library of new bestsellers and classics that can be immediately obtained and downloaded to your Mac.

Downloading Books

Open the iBooks app from your Applications folder and sign in using your Apple ID. You'll be shown your book library, which will include those already purchased using your login on other devices. From there it's straightforward. You can see charts, featured titles, bestseller lists and there's the facility to search.

Once you've found your title you can choose to buy the whole book or buy a sample. Usually the publisher grants a sizeable excerpt or the first chapter or two free of charge, or you can

Hot Tip

If you already own an Amazon Kindle reader or have non-Apple mobile devices, you're better off downloading the free, cross-platform Kindle App for your Mac to ensure your purchases are available on all of your devices.

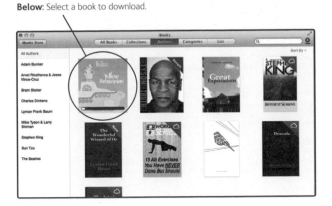

Below: Select a book to download.

just buy the whole thing straight off. Selecting either option will download it to your iBooks app.

Free Books

Ebooks can be really, really expensive given you don't get anything physical for your money, but did you know the world is awash with classics you can download for free because the copyright has expired? Enter the Free Books section of iBooks and you'll see the likes of Sherlock Holmes, *The Wizard Of Oz* and *Pride And Prejudice* available, free of charge.

Reading Books In iBooks

Reading an entire book on your Mac isn't the greatest experience in all honesty; they're better suited to mobile devices. However, it does work and can be handy if you're working on an essay and need to reference elements of the book. Here are a few basics.

- **Turn pages**: Move the arrow keys left and right.

- **Highlight text**: Hold the mouse/trackpad button down where you want to begin highlighting and drag the trackpad to the end of the section.

- **Copying text**: Hit Command + C.

- **Pasting text in another app**: Command + V.

- **Annotate text**: Highlight section, select Notes from the pop-up window and begin typing.

- **Highlight text**: Highlight the section and choose a colour.

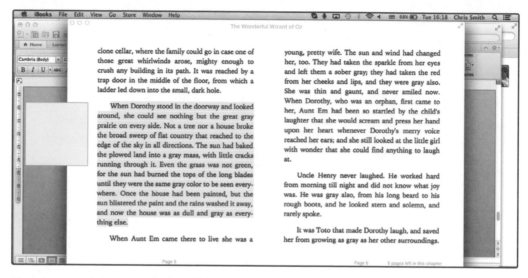

Above: You can use the mouse or trackpad to highlight text. The notepad icon allows you to access these later.

- **Access Notes/Highlights:** Click the notepad icon in the toolbar.

- **Look up text:** Highlight text, select More and choose from web, Wikipedia or the rest of the book to load results.

- **Dictionary search:** Double tap on a word.

- **Change font/size/style:** Hit the double A icon in the toolbar.

- **Search for text:** Hit the magnifying class and begin typing in the field.

- **Add bookmarks:** Hitting the bookmark icon in the toolbar turns it red, saving the page. Hitting the drop-down arrow next to it shows all bookmarks.

Hot Tip

To zoom in and out on text, hit Command along with the plus or minus key on the keyboard.

GETTING CREATIVE WITH YOUR MAC

As we mentioned earlier in the book, the great creative tools are a one of the key motivations for people buying Macs. Right out of the box, your computer comes with some simple yet powerful tools to help you create your own movies and music.

GARAGEBAND

GarageBand is one of the most popular Apple-made apps ever. It allows you to create entire songs on your Mac, complete with percussion, vocals, effects and much more. You don't need to know how to read or play music to create a song. If you can? You can plug your guitar in and record a riff directly on to your Mac.

Above: GarageBand is an incredibly popular app which allows you to make music on your Mac.

iMOVIE

Just as iPhoto lets you work wonders with your photographs, iMovie allows you to turn your home movies into fully edited projects, complete with audio, effects, captions and more. Then you can share them with family and friends or upload on to YouTube for the whole world to enjoy.

Hot Tip

For more apps for creative types, check out our 100 Top Apps on pages 252–253.

NETWORKING AND SHARING

GETTING ONLINE AT HOME AND IN PUBLIC

It may sound obvious, but your Mac isn't able to magically connect to the Internet without the presence of some external factors. In this section we'll guide you through the complexities of the connected home.

WHAT YOU'LL NEED

As we discussed back at the beginning, each Mac you buy is capable of connecting to wireless and wired Internet networks, but to make that happen at home you'll need a few additional things at your disposal.

Above: You will need a live broadband account in order to connect your Mac to the Internet.

A Live Broadband Account

Unless you have a live account with an Internet provider, such BT, Sky, Virgin, TalkTalk and the like, then you won't be getting on the Internet. These ISPs (Internet service providers) offer contracts at a monthly rate, where you'll be able to select the speed of your connection and the amount of data you'll be allowed to download. The package you choose will depend on mainly two factors.

1. How many devices (tablets, phones, computers, speakers, printers, etc.) do you wish to connect to the network? The more devices, the larger the load the network must cope with.

2. What will you use your connection for? Downloading and streaming lots of media? You'll want faster speeds and potentially unlimited data. Casually browsing the web and sending emails? You can get away with modest speeds and data allowance.

Broadband Equipment

Your Mac has everything inside to connect to the Internet, but wherever you connect there'll need to be some sort of Internet receiver. In the home this usually translates to a wireless broadband modem. This will be supplied by the company you sign up with. You can have them come and install if you wish, or they'll send you the modem with an easy set-up guide. You'll be online and surfing quick as a flash.

Above: Broadband providers will supply a wireless modem when you sign up and can also install it for you.

A Home Phone Landline

While this is not always the case, most ISPs also require you to have a live BT phone line. The exception is Virgin, which offers fibre-optic cable broadband. It is not available in all areas, so check online.

Below: An Ethernet adapter.

Ethernet Cable

If you wish to physically connect to the Internet rather than wirelessly, you'll need one of these strange, thick cables running between your modem and your Mac. On most new MacBook models an Ethernet port has been sacrificed in order to save space, so you'll need an adapter, like the one pictured here. They're £25/$29 from Apple.

GETTING ONLINE

Now the home is configured we can jump online. Here's a quick guide to connecting to your home network, if you didn't already do so when setting up your Mac.

CONNECTING WIRELESSLY TO YOUR HOME NETWORK

If you have a live broadband account and a wireless modem (they mostly all are these days), you'll be able to connect to Wi-Fi. Apple's new MacBooks are equipped with 'AirPort' wireless cards that allow you to connect to the Internet via radio signals when paired with a nearby router.

The first step is to identify the name of the network you're connecting to. It'll be identified on your modem as the network ID. Usually it'll consist of the name of your broadband provider together with a combination of letters and numbers (for example BTHomeHub2-HM26).

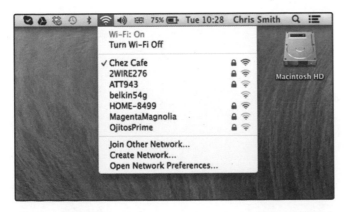

Step 3: Select the correct network ID from the drop-down menu.

1. Hit the Internet signal icon in your Mac's menu bar. If you're not connected, it'll be empty.

2. If Wi-Fi is noted as Off, turn it On.

3. The list of networks in range will appear in the drop-down menu. Choose the network ID that corresponds with your home network (see above).

4. Enter the password. This will also be given on the modem.

From now on your Mac will remember this and automatically connect to this network whenever you're in range. This enables you to wander around your house without being tethered by wires.

The Importance Of The Password

Ensure you always keep your network password safe and secure to prevent other people (neighbours, perhaps) from jumping on to your network. Password settings can be altered by logging into your modem. Contact your ISP and find out the unique IP address for that modem and type this into your web browser. You'll also need an admin password (it's usually 'admin'). Once you're in, you can change the network password to something stronger, rather than the generic network key shown on the modem.

Staying Wired

If your Mac is likely to stay in one place, like on your desk, then you may want to employ a wired connection to the network. All new Macs have lightning-fast gigabit Ethernet connections, which means you'll be able to harness the full power of your network speed. It's also easier to set up and more secure than wireless networks. You can achieve this by using the aforementioned Ethernet cables and plugging them into your Mac and the modem. This should automatically connect you to the network.

If not, run the Assist Me tool in Network Preferences or go to the Troubleshooting section that deals with the Internet on page 212.

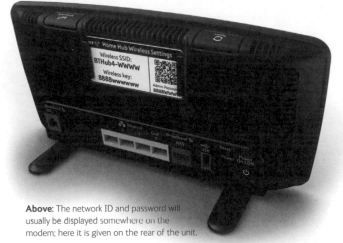

Am I Connected?

There are a few ways to check that you're online. The easiest is to open Safari and browse to a webpage. If that page loads, well, it's safe to say you're online. You can also head to System Preferences > Network. If the green light in the sidebar is lit, then you're online. If you see red or amber lights, you may be connected to a network itself, but without access to the Internet. We'll deal with that in the final Troubleshooting chapter (see page 212).

Above: The network ID and password will usually be displayed somewhere on the modem; here it is given on the rear of the unit.

CONNECTING TO A PUBLIC NETWORK WIRELESSLY

If you snapped up a MacBook Air or a MacBook Pro, the chances are you're going to be using it on the go, in the office, at friends' houses, and in cafés and coffee shops around town. Here are a few tips to help you out.

Public Networks And Passwords

There are few differences between connecting wirelessly at home and in public. The main difference comes in the password situation. Workplaces and smaller businesses will likely password-protect their networks. In this case you'll need to request the password from the premises' IT guys or the staff with the password.

On other occasions, in larger chains like the Starbuckses and Costas of this world, you'll connect to the network in the normal manner; when you see a pop-up web window you'll have to accept some terms and conditions and then you'll be permitted to get online. Some providers like 'The Cloud' offer free or limited Internet access, but you'll need to sign up for an account when you log in.

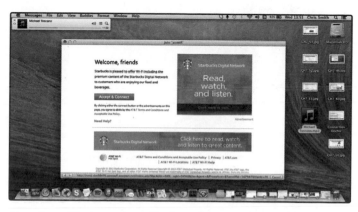

Above: Some public places, such as coffee shops, offer a wireless internet connection.

Protect Your Mac On A Public Network

A network wouldn't be a network unless multiple devices were involved. This can be great when accessing content across devices on your own network, but in the public domain, you'll want to ensure your Mac's content is hidden from prying eyes. The easiest way to do this is to go to System Preferences > Sharing and make sure File Sharing does not have a tick box next to it.

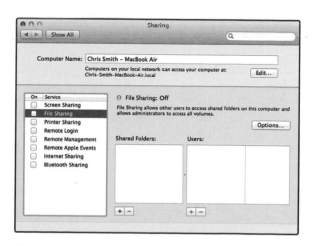

Above: When using public networks, File Sharing should be turned off.

OTHER WAYS TO CONNECT TO THE INTERNET

While Wi-Fi networks and Ethernet are the two most likely ways you'll get online, there are alternative ways to connect your Mac to the Internet.

Mobile Broadband Dongle

If you don't want to sign up for a lengthy broadband contract and only intend to be a light user, you may wish to consider a mobile broadband dongle available from networks like O2, Three, EE and Vodafone. They plug directly into your Mac's USB port. These can be bought as pay-as-you-go data packages meaning you aren't committed to a monthly outlay. They're easy enough to set up, (just plug in the device and install the software when prompted) and connect.

Smartphone Tethering With Mobile Hotspots

Did you know your bundled smartphone data can be used as a mobile hotspot? This can sometimes be used to get online when there is no access to wired/Wi-Fi Internet, when you're in the park or at the beach.

Hot Tip

If you're using mobile tethering, be sure not to blow all of your data in one fell swoop. No downloading big movie files from iTunes!

Depending on your phone and provider, you can switch on the Wi-Fi hotspot functionality and piggyback on the 3G/4G connections. Some networks will make you buy an additional data bundle to enable Internet tethering, while others offer the bundle for free. Once the hotspot is set up and enabled, you'll be able to access the network in the usual way.

Above: Wi-Fi hotspot on a phone.

USING AN AIRPORT EXPRESS MODEM

Although your own modem is perfectly capable of getting you online, Apple sells its own router, called the AirPort Express. It can be configured easily using your network settings and by plugging into your existing modem via an Ethernet cable. It is a completely non-essential purchase, but can assist your home network in a number of ways.

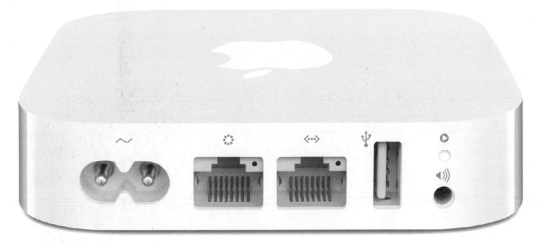

Above: A set of powered speakers or a USB printer can be connected to the AirPort Express, to make them WI-FI enabled.

Expand Your Musical Reach With AirPort Express

With an AirPort Express modem, you can turn a set of powered speakers (not USB) into Wi-Fi enabled speakers. By hooking them up to the AirPort Express with a 3.5-mm cable, you can send music from iTunes on your Mac via AirPlay (see page 172). This is also handy if you have speakers in another room.

Make A USB Printer Wireless

A USB printer can be plugged into the AirPort Express, turning it into a wireless printer, to which you can send documents from anywhere in the home. Just plug the printer into the USB port and print over Wi-Fi to the AirPort Express.

Setting Up An AirPort Express With AirPort Utility

Within your Mac's Utilities folder within Applications, you'll find AirPort Utility, which allows you to control the AirPort Express router's settings. Here you'll be able to configure your network settings by joining your existing network or setting up a new one.

1. Plug your new AirPort Express base station into the mains.

2. Run an Ethernet cable from your base station to your Internet modem.

3. Give it a few seconds to settle in. The light should flash green as it sets up, and then show solid orange to indicate there's no active connection.

4. Open AirPort Utility on your Mac.

5. If you have an old version, you'll be asked to update. Do this.

6. The AirPort Utility app should recognize the AirPort Express. Select it and hit Continue. If not, select 'Other Wi-Fi devices' where it may appear.

7. Once it is selected it'll attempt to configure your network settings. You can create a New AirPort Express network or configure it with your existing network.

8. If adding it to an existing network, you'll need to select your router name; just click the base station name and enter your network's password.

9. It'll take a few minutes and your modem may reset itself in the meantime, but once the process is complete you'll see a green light on the base station and within AirPort Utility.

10. From there, you're good to begin connecting a USB printer or a set of speakers to your AirPort Express.

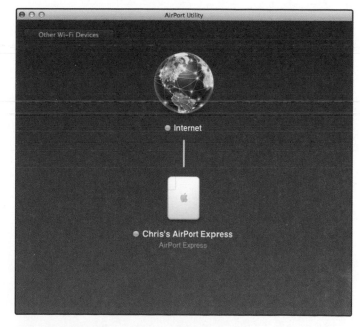

Step 6: The AirPort Utility app should recognize the AirPort Express.

SHARING FILES AND INTERNET CONNECTIONS

Did you know you can share your Mac's Internet connection with other poor Internet-less souls and create a network of your own to share files with other Macs?

CREATING A WI-FI HOTSPOT FROM YOUR WIRED MAC

Now the circumstances in which you'll use this feature may be quite rare, but it's handy nonetheless. If your Mac is connected to a wired modem and there's no Wi-Fi available, you can make that connection available to other devices. Essentially, it turns your Mac into a wireless router.

Step 5: Tick the Internet Sharing box and then click Start.

1. Head to System Preferences > Sharing.

2. Ensure 'Ethernet' is selected from the 'Share your connection from' menu.

3. Select Wi-Fi from the 'to computers using' section.

4. Select Internet Options (Wi-Fi Options in Mavericks) from the bottom right of the screen. Here, you'll be able to choose a name and set a password for your network. Hit OK.

5. From the left side of the screen tick the Internet Sharing box and select Start.

6. Now other devices will be able to connect to your network using the password you provide them with.

7. Internet Sharing can be turned off at any time by unticking the box within the Sharing portion of system preferences.

CREATING COMPUTER-TO-COMPUTER NETWORKS

There are plenty of ways to share files over the Internet, which we'll go into later in this chapter, but did you know you can also create a network between two or more devices to transfer files if there is no network connectivity present? The process is quite similar to creating the Wi-Fi hotspot shown above.

1. In the menu bar hit the AirPort icon and select Create Network from the drop-down menu.

2. Name the network (don't worry about the Channel) and create a password. This is important. Otherwise anyone will be able to jump on, and that you do not want.

3. The password must be made up of 10 hex digits (the letters A–F and the numbers 0–9).

4. Select Create.

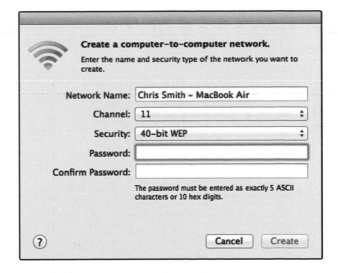

Step 3: Choose a name for the network and then create a password which is made up of 10 hex digits.

5. You'll see the AirPort icon in the menu bar replaced by a computer. You won't be able to use the Internet at this time.

6. You, or another user, can connect to this network in the conventional way. You'll now be able to connect to and access each other's files in the Shared section of the Finder window.

SHARING FILES OVER THE NETWORK

If you're using several computers over one network, or wish to share files with colleagues on the network, you can configure your Mac to make files available publicly over the Internet connection. Firstly, you need to head to System Preferences > Sharing and enable File Sharing by ticking the box in the sidebar.

This enables Mac and Windows users to view pre-determined files and folders on your network. To add which folders you wish to share, you can click the +/− buttons next to shared folders. While those settings are enabled, these files can be accessed by other users.

Hot Tip

If you only wish to share certain files, create a folder on your desktop, place the files you wish to share in it and make that a shared folder by selecting it, tapping the shortcut Control + I and hitting the Shared Folder tick box.

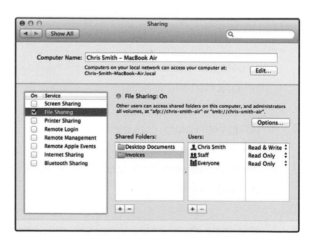

Above: Enable File Sharing to allow other users to view certain folders.

Accessing Shared Files On Other Computers

Just as you're able to make your files available to be shared on public networks, you can also browse to files on other Windows or Mac computers that have been made publicly available. If these computers are on the same network, you'll see them represented within the Shared sidebar in the Finder window. You can browse and open these files as you would when browsing your own computer.

Sharing Screens

Did you know it's possible to share your screen with other computers on the network? To share your screen is to allow others to see what you're working on and for them to remotely control apps and documents on your screen with their computer.

1. To allow access to your screen, head to System Preferences > Sharing and tick the Screen Sharing box in the sidebar.

2. In the Allow Access section you can allow anyone with a user account on your computer to take control, or select which users you'd like to have access.

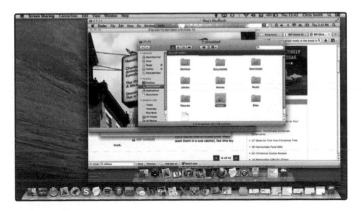

Above: You can share your screen with other users and allow them to control it remotely.

3. To set up permissions, click the Computer Settings button. Here you can ensure users have to ask permission to access the screen (you'll get a notification you'll need to accept), or you can set up a password.

4. If other users are on a Mac, they'll see your screen in the Shared Devices area in Finder. Likewise, you'll find access to shared screens in your own Finder window.

Borrowing Another Mac's Optical Disc Drive

As we've already mentioned, some Mac models have dispensed with the CD/DVD drive to save space. If you really need to play a DVD, burn a CD or install disc-based software on your Mac, you can borrow another machine's drive rather than buying a USB Superdrive (*see* page 26). Before you begin, you need to check both computers are on the same network.

1. If you're sharing another Mac drive, head to System Preferences > Sharing on that Mac and tick CD/DVD sharing. You can choose whether permission is needed.

2. On the Mac that's doing the sharing, you should see a Remote Disc show up in the Finder window.

3. Browse to Remote Disc and double click the icon for the first Mac. If you chose to request permission, you can request it and then click on Accept on the other device.

4. Now you can use a disc as if it were inside your own computer.

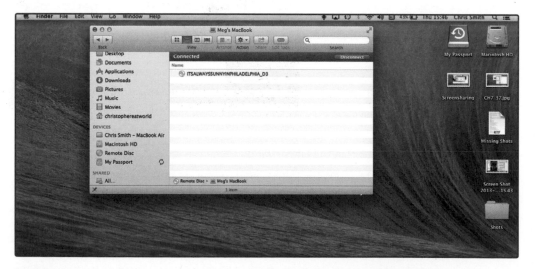

Above: If your own Mac does not have an optical drive, it is possible to share the drive of another Mac on the network.

AIRDROP

AirDrop is another one of those handy Mac-to-Mac features (introduced with Mac OS X Lion), and is probably the easiest way for Mac users in the same vicinity to share content with each other. In this case the Macs don't have to be running on the same Wi-Fi network. As well as sharing files with each other, this can be handy for exchanging files between your own Macs, if you have more than one.

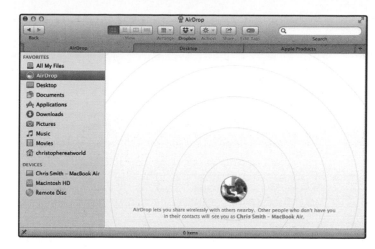

Above: AirDrop is an easy way to share content between Macs which are close to each other.

Sharing Files With AirDrop

There are a few ways to share files, folders, text and so on using AirDrop. You'll find it within the Finder sidebar under Favorites or can access it by selecting Finder > Go > AirDrop. Whichever you choose, the Finder window will now search for other Macs running AirDrop in the vicinity.

Hot Tip

Files can also be shared with AirDrop by selecting them in a Finder window and selecting AirDrop from the Share button menu.

Once the Macs are showing within the Finder window, you can drag and drop any files you wish on to that user's profile picture, then press Send to process the request. Once the other user has accepted, the transfer will begin.

Receiving Files Via AirDrop

In order to receive files via AirDrop you just need to have it activated in a Finder window. When other Mac users send you a request, you'll be asked to accept the transfer.

Step 2: The Mac will search for other devices which are in range.

Step 4: Select the device to connect to and then click Pair.

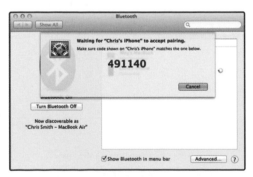

Step 5: Before a device is finally paired, the recipient will have to accept.

B IS FOR BLUETOOTH

With all of these fancy means of sharing over Wi-Fi using AirDrop, AirPlay and more, poor old Bluetooth has taken a back seat in recent years. However, the short-range connectivity tech is still built into all Macs, PCs and most mobile devices. It's handy for pairing peripherals like keyboards, mice and printers, and exchanging files over short distances.

Pairing Up Devices Via Bluetooth

First of all, ensure the device you want to pair with is switched on and has Bluetooth switched on and in discoverable mode. Without that you might as well not bother.

1. Turn on Bluetooth on your Mac by selecting the B icon in the menu bar.

2. Open Bluetooth preferences and your Mac will search for the discoverable devices that are in range.

3. You may see other keyboards, phones, tablets, speakers, printers and other devices depending on your location and set-up.

4. Select the device and click Pair. The Mac will examine the device and find the best way to communicate with it. Usually it will send users a keycode to type in or accept.

5. The device will then show as connected. Double click it to send files. The recipient will need to accept.

Pairing A Wireless Keyboard And Trackpad

We dealt with this briefly during set-up in Chapter Two, for wireless peripherals that were pre-paired with your Mac. If you want to buy and pair new ones, it's easily done.

1. Turn on the keyboard/trackpad via the button at the side.

2. Browse to System Preferences and select Keyboard/Trackpad, then Set Up Bluetooth Keyboard/Trackpad.

3. It'll take a couple of seconds to discover the keyboard. Once it appears, hit Continue.

4. If it's a keyboard you'll need to enter an eight-digit passcode. In the case of a trackpad it should automatically pair.

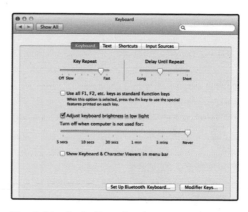

Step 2: Select Set Up Bluetooth Keyboard/Trackpad.

Sending Audio To Bluetooth Speakers

Bluetooth speakers are still quite popular and are certainly more abundant than those with AirPlay functionality (see page 176). To pair with Bluetooth speakers, follow the steps above. Then select System Preferences > Sound and select the speaker as the Output Device. This will ensure all audio is played through the external speakers.

Above: Bluetooth speakers can be set as the Output Device.

SHARING MEDIA FILES AND STREAMING CONTENT

Now all of the geeky networking stuff is out of the way, we can get on to some more enjoyable tasks, like beaming music, video and your screen to other devices via AirPlay.

Above: Click the AirPlay logo within iTunes to see the various options.

AIRPLAY

The Apple-to-Apple streaming technology is one of those neat tricks the company pulls to keep you within its ecosystem and exclusively using its gadgets. An AirPlay-enabled home, complete with like-minded devices, can revolutionize how you experience entertainment content. Over Wi-Fi you can beam content to the TV or a pair of speakers from your Mac and iOS devices.

APPLE TV

The Apple TV is a neat, fairly inexpensive (£100/$100) device resembling a hockey puck that plugs into your HD TV via the HDMI port. It enables you to rent movies and TV shows over the Internet and is also capable of streaming live and on-demand content from apps like Netflix, Sky News and the like. However, for our purposes it's most useful due to its ability to communicate wirelessly with your Mac and beam media to your television set.

Above: Apple TV can communicate wirelessly with your Mac and beam media to the TV.

Streaming Music/Video With Apple TV

If you're on the same Wi-Fi or wired network as an AirPlay-enabled device like the Apple TV box, you're able to share iTunes media with that device.

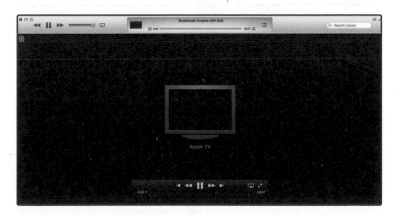

Above: With Apple TV, media from iTunes can be played through the television.

Within iTunes, you'll see the AirPlay icon pictured. Click this icon and select Apple TV. Start playing your music or video in iTunes and within a few seconds you'll get audio and video coming through your television and its sound system. You can use the media controls on your Mac or the Apple TV remote to control playback.

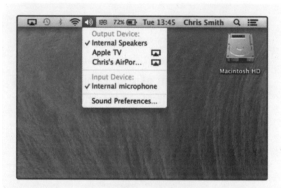

Hot Tip

To share your computer's audio, from any application to an AirPlay-enabled device, hold down the Option key, click the volume indicator in the menu bar and select the relevant device.

AirPlay Mirroring

It's not just music and video you can send to an Apple TV box; if you want, you can send your whole screen wirelessly to your television using AirPlay Mirroring.

This allows you to view what you're doing on a larger screen (great if you're giving presentations or watching a video stream over the Internet), but also to extend your desktop to another screen so windows can be dragged on to the TV without plugging in an external cable. Here's how it's done.

1. To access AirPlay Mirroring, hit the AirPlay icon in the menu bar and select Apple TV under Connect to AirPlay Display.

2. This will turn the AirPlay icon blue and your desktop should now show up on your television.

3. Once you're connected, click the AirPlay icon again. Here you can select whether you want to 'Mirror Built in Display' or 'Extend Desktop'.

> ## Hot Tip
> **Want to show off a photo slideshow on your TV? Use AirPlay Mirroring to connect to your TV. Open iPhoto, find the album of your choice and hit Play Slideshow.**

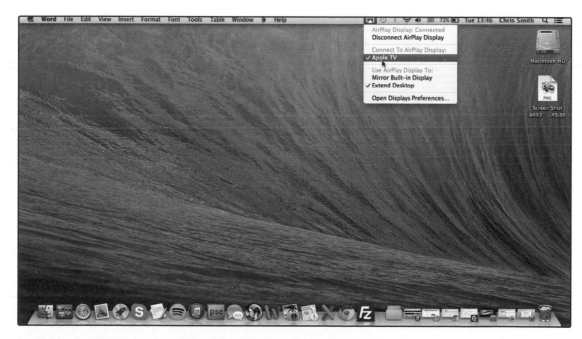

Step 1: Select the AirPlay icon from the menu bar, and from the drop-down menu, select Apple TV.

4. This will automatically send audio to the Apple TV.

5. To turn off AirPlay Mirroring, click the blue AirPlay icon and hit Disconnect.

Other AirPlay-enabled Devices

If you want to stream music from your Mac (or iPhone, iPod touch or iPad for that matter) to a set of speakers, one option is to buy an AirPlay-enabled set of speakers. There are more and more on offer, but here are some of the most popular models.

- The B&W Zeppelin 2 or B&W Zeppelin Air (bowers-wilkins.com).

- Bose Soundlink Air Digital Music (Bose.com).

- Cambridge Audio Minx Air 200 (CambridgeAudio.com).

- Loewe AirSpeaker (loewe.tv).

Hot Tip

Got some old speakers that you want to use to play music wirelessly? Connecting an AirPort Express to a pair of powered speakers makes them AirPlay compatible (*see* page 161).

Connecting A Second Monitor

If you're not using an AirPlay-enabled display you can easily connect one using the requisite cables. That could mean using another computer on your desk to give you more screen space to work, or simply hooking up to the TV via HDMI to watch content on a bigger screen. Once you're connected, head to Displays in System Preferences to configure.

iTUNES HOME SHARING

iTunes Home Sharing is a pre-cursor to AirPlay, but remains very important. It makes all of your media files

Above: You can share your entire iTunes library with other devices on the same Wi-Fi network.

available across a Wi-Fi network. It allows you to access your Mac's entire iTunes media library on up to five different computers, iOS devices or an Apple TV device. In essence it's a great way to share your library without having to store the files on multiple devices.

Setting Up iTunes Home Sharing

First of all, open iTunes and head to Preferences. Head to Sharing and select the tick box next to Share your home library on my local network. Here you can choose to share the entire library or just certain playlists. Once selected, those files will be available for playback within the devices listed above.

- **On other computers:** Open iTunes. The shared library will appear beneath the 'Shared' section of the sidebar.

- **On iOS devices:** Head to the Music/Video apps, select More > Shared.

- **On Apple TV:** Go to the Computers app where you'll see the shared iTunes library.

Above: The Mac's iTunes library shared to an iPhone.

PRINTING, SCANNING AND EXTERNAL DISPLAYS

Although the dominance of email has lessened the need for physical documents, a printer and scanner are still a necessity in some homes and offices. Here are some tips on adding more devices and displays to your network.

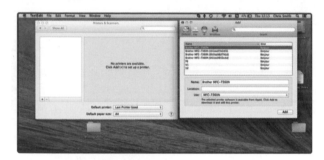

Above: Select the printer you have connected to your Mac.

CONNECTING A PRINTER TO YOUR MAC

Once, you had no choice but to tether your Mac physically to the printer via a component cable or USB. Now there are some other options, thanks to wireless technologies like Bluetooth and Wi-Fi.

USB Printers

If you're keeping your Mac on your desk, this might be the simplest and most reliable option. Connect your printer to the mains and turn it on. Connect the USB cable to both devices. It's likely that your Mac already contains the 'driver' software necessary to run it.

Wi-Fi-Enabled Printers And AirPrint

AirPrint allows you to print documents wirelessly over your Wi-Fi network from your Mac or iOS mobile devices.

Currently there are over 700 AirPrint-compatible printers available for your Mac from around 16 manufacturers. Apple keeps a list on its website (http://support.apple.com/kb/HT4356). Set up your printer using the instructions provided and connect to the Wi-Fi network.

Setting Up A Bluetooth Printer

We dealt with Bluetooth earlier in this section and you can pair up the device using the method shown on page 170.

Adding Printers To Your Network

Regardless of how you're hooking up your printers, you'll need to go to System

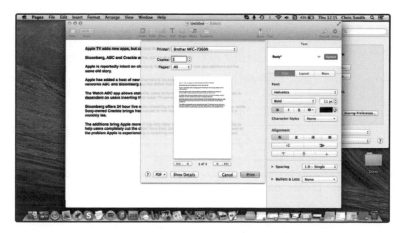

Above: Attempt to print a document: if no printer is listed, you will need to add one.

Preferences > Printers & Scanners to configure the device. Hit the + button to search for the printer. It should pop up in the list, allowing you to add it to the network. Alternatively, you can attempt to print a document (Command + P). If no printer is listed, hit Add Printer to find nearby or connectable printers.

Hot Tip

To share your printer with other Macs across the network, allowing other computers to use it, select the printer in System Preferences and tick 'Share this printer on the network'.

PRINTING ON MACS

In most document-creation and viewing apps on your Mac (the likes of Pages, Preview, Safari) you access the print settings in the File section of the menu bar or by hitting the shortcut Command + P.

Mastering The Print Settings

Before your document starts printing, you'll be asked to confirm a host of settings: layout, orientation, paper size, page range, number of copies, colour and paper choices. Select Show Details to configure the settings to your preference. Hit Print, and you're good to go.

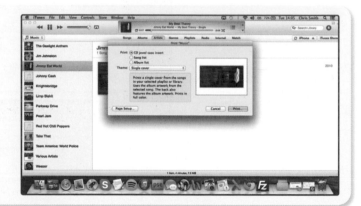

Hot Tip

If you plan on burning an album or playlist to a CD in iTunes, you can easily print a case insert by hitting Command + P and selecting Print jewel case insert.

USING SCANNERS

'A scanner?' you ask. 'What is this? 1997? Who uses scanners?' Yes, we know, but wait until you have to print and sign an important document and get it back to the sender within the hour. Then you'll realize why this section is here.

Hooking Up A Scanner To Your Mac

A lot of modern printers have scanners built into them, so if you have one of these all-in-one multi-taskers, then you don't need to worry. If you have a standalone model, it's likely you'll hook it up via USB. Once it is connected, your Mac should recognize it and you're good to go.

Scanning In Documents

We haven't discussed it yet, but there's a dedicated app called Image Capture that's perfect for this business. Load it up and follow the steps.

1. Open the Image Capture app and place the document or photo face down on the scanning bed, so it's facing the glass surface.

2. Alternatively, if the scanner features a document feeder, you can feed it into the scanner.

3. Click Scan and Image Capture will automatically scan the document. You can choose whether you 'Detect Separate Items' in order to capture other aspects of the page.

4. Select 'Scan To' to save the scanned document to a location of your choosing.

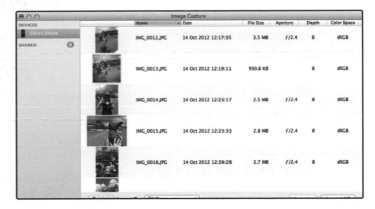

Above: Image Capture is a dedicated app for scanning documents in to your Mac.

Hot Tip

To make corrections to the scanned document, open Preview and select Import From Scanner to open the file.

PROTECTING YOUR MAC

BACKING UP YOUR FILES

Somewhere around the turn of the century the excuse 'my hard drive failed' replaced 'the dog ate my homework'; only this time it was true! In this section we'll examine the plentiful tools available to Mac users to ensure they never lose work, media files or memories.

WHY BACK UP YOUR COMPUTER?

For every way there is to back up your data, there's a really good reason to do so. Before we delve into how to do it, here are just four reasons to ensure your data is safe at all times.

1. If you lose your Mac or it is stolen, your vital work documents are secured elsewhere in the iCloud or on hard drives ... that's if you backed up, of course.

2. If your Mac dies an untimely death, via accident or hardware failure, your photo and music collections do not have to die with it. They can easily be restored to a new machine ... if you took the time to back up.

Above: Recover mistakenly deleted files with Time Machine.

3. If you can't take your Mac with you everywhere, you can always access that office presentation, spreadsheet or your CV. That's if you backed up.

4. If you desperately need to return to an earlier time period, before you deleted your work files by accident, you can access it via your Time Machine. Only if you backed up, though.

Backing Up Using An External Hard Drive

Probably the easiest way to safeguard your files is to copy them over to an external hard drive, which can be transported around with you. External hard drives are relatively inexpensive with a massive 1 Terabyte USB hard drive costing around £50 ($70), right down to small USB memory sticks, which can be no more expensive than a couple of quid.

1. In order to copy files from your Mac to a USB hard drive, simply plug it in to the USB port on your Mac.

2. The disc image should appear on your desktop.

3. Open the disc in a Finder window.

4. Select and copy (Command + C) the files/folders you wish to back up and paste (Command + V) them within the new disc. Alternatively, drag and drop them.

Above: The external hard drive will appear in your Finder window.

5.　Wait until the progress bar indicates that the file transfer is complete.

6.　Be sure to hit the eject icon in Finder, or right click and select Eject to ensure the hard drive is ejected safely.

Hot Tip

For way, way faster file transfers, get yourself a Thunderbolt external hard drive, providing your Mac has a Thunderbolt port, that is.

Freeing Up Space With An External Hard Drive

Your Mac's hard drive can get really full, really quickly, especially if you have a large media collection. You can free up some space by moving files you don't access very often to an external hard drive for safekeeping.

1. To move files off your hard drive and on to an external hard drive, plug the drive in via the USB port and open it in a Finder window.

2. Select the files you wish to copy and move them onto the new hard drive as outlined previously.

3. Wait for the file transfer to complete and check they're sitting on the drive before ejecting the drive (*see left*).

4. Move all of the copied files on your Mac to Trash and empty to delete permanently.

Hot Tip

Naturally these files can be moved back on to your Mac at any time, or simply accessed, modified and saved back to the external drive.

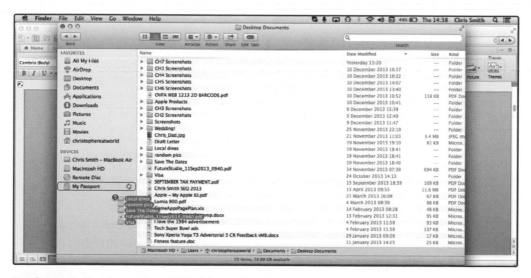

Step 2: Select the files to be copied on to the hard drive, and drag them across to move them.

YOUR VERY OWN TIME MACHINE

For the smartest and most diligent back-up artists, Apple's Time Machine functionality is king. Not only does it back up the state of your entire Mac to an external hard drive, but it does so automatically on a scheduled basis and knows about all the changes you make. The idea is that you can revisit your Mac at a certain point in time and access lost, damaged or changed files. Even your favourite settings are saved.

Above: Time Machine allows access to previous points in time in your Mac's history.

Choosing A Hard Drive

You can use any compatible, dedicated USB hard drive to configure Time Machine. Providing there's enough space, it'll back up the contents of your Mac on a scheduled basis, providing it's plugged into your computer.

The Apple Time Capsule

The Dom Perignon of back-up drives is the Apple AirPort Time Capsule. Not only is it a wireless base station with all of the functionality of the AirPort Express (see page 161), but it also features up to 3 TB of storage to wirelessly back up your Mac using Time Machine.

It's easy to set up and is the 100 per cent worry-free option. However, this drive or the peace of mind it brings doesn't come terribly cheaply. The 2 TB Time Capsule currently costs around £249/$299.

Setting Up Time Machine

First of all you'll need to open the Time Machine program and select a drive location for your back-ups. You'll find it within the Applications folder and in System Preferences.

1. Open the app and select Set Up Time Machine.

2. Turn Time Machine ON and you'll be prompted to select your Backup Disk.

3. Select the USB or Thunderbolt (or Firewire if you're using an older Mac) drive physically connected to the Mac or the Time Capsule drive if you splashed out.

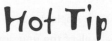

Hot Tip

If you have an AirPort Extreme base station, it supports USB hard drives. Plug this in and use it as you would a wireless Apple Time Capsule.

Step 1: Open the Time Machine app.

Step 2: Select the drive to save the back-up data to.

Step 3: Time Machine will now prepare to back up your Mac.

4. If you're using a physical hard drive it may ask you erase the content currently on the drive because of an incompatible file system. Be sure there's nothing important on the drive before you click Erase.

5. Once you've set up the Time Machine, the app will begin backing up your data. It will take a few hours to complete.

Scheduling Time Machine Back-ups

Providing your Time Capsule is connected to the network or your external hard drive is connected to your computer, the Time Machine app will begin by backing up your data every hour. Over time it will store hourly back-ups for the last 24 hours, daily back-ups for the past month and weekly back-ups for all previous months. This means you'll be able to go back in time and access a version of your computer from any given week. Once the disc is full, the oldest versions will be deleted.

Hot Tip
If you wish to perform a back-up manually, say if you need to remove the external hard drive, hit the Time Machine logo that appears in the menu bar and hit Back Up Now.

Above: Search through the stack of Finder windows to find old files.

Working With Time Machine

Now your Mac is backing itself up on the hour, every hour, you've got your very own DeLorean. Hit the Time Machine icon in the menu bar and select Enter Time Machine. This will whisk away all of your other windows and present you with a mountain of Finder windows stacked on top of each other. You can search within these Finder windows and move back and forth between them using the arrows at the foot of the screen to find your files. Once you've found the file, hit Restore and it'll be brought back to the present.

Above: To set up further preferences, click Options at the bottom right of the Time Machine app.

Time Machine Options

There are a couple of extra bits and bobs regarding Time Machine you should know about. These sit within Options in the Time Machine. If you hit the tick box 'Back up when running off battery' It may take a bigger toll on battery life. Also, you can choose to be notified when older back-ups are deleted within this menu.

Hot Tip

Before you back up you'll be notified about the estimated size of the back-up. Make sure you have a hard drive large enough for the job.

BACKING UP WITH DISK UTILITY

Disk Utility will come in very handy later when we're troubleshooting, but it's also handy for backing up, burning and archiving some of the files on your Mac.

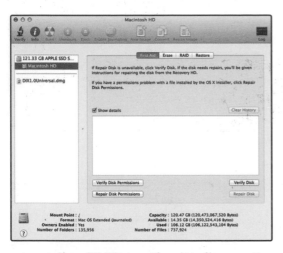

Above: Disk Utility is great for archiving files on your Mac.

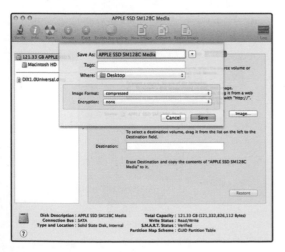

Step 4: Choose a name for the folder and where to save it.

Create Disk Image

Another way to archive files on your Mac is to use the Disk Utility application to create what's known as a 'disc image'. This allows you to create a virtual second hard drive within your Mac, where material you don't use very often can be compressed and stored in order to save space, and encrypted to keep out prying eyes. These compressed folders can then be burned to discs, moved to different hard drives or sent to other Mac users.

1. Move all of the files you want to archive into a folder.

2. Open the Utilities folder and select Disk Utility.

3. Hit File > New > New From Folder and select your folder in Finder.

4. Choose a name for the folder, choose a destination to save it, and whether you wish to compress it.

5. Choose the level of encryption and select a password. This will be needed to open the Disk Image in the future. Don't lose this password.

6. Once the image has been created, it is yours to do with as you will.

BURNING TO DISC

It's also possible to store your files on CD/DVD by burning them from your hard drive. You'll need blank, writeable discs and an optical drive to put them in.

1. Place the disc in the optical drive to load an open Finder window.

2. Simply drag and drop the files you want to store.

3. Hit the Burn icon when you're finished.

Alternatively, you can go through the Disk Instructions listed to the left, and then simply hit Burn when the image has been created.

Complete Back-ups

There are several third-party applications that allow you to back up absolutely everything on your Mac, if disaster strikes and you need to restore from scratch. Try Carbon Copy Cloner or Crashplan.

THE POWER OF THE CLOUD

More and more people are choosing to utilize the cloud as a way to store and back up their files on the Internet. Using services like iCloud and Dropbox, among others, makes it easy to automatically save files and access them on multiple devices.

APPLE iCLOUD

We've talked extensively about iCloud in the book so far. This online storage solution pops up in several of the applications we've discussed, like Pages, iTunes, Safari, Calendar, iPhoto, Maps and more. The service is now an integral part of the Mac experience. Here's how to get the best out of it.

Above: iCloud works with files from various applications.

What Does iCloud Back Up?

iCloud is not a traditional back-up service. It's not really about transferring files for access later, it's more about keeping your information up to date and making it available across your devices. It's something that, once set up, you won't really think about using. For example:

1. Photos imported into iPhoto can be automatically sent to Photo Streams. This doesn't even count towards your free 5 GB storage!

2. Calendar events created on your Mac are synced to your iOS devices.

3. Music you've bought from iTunes will be instantly available to download on other devices with iCloud.

Signing Into iCloud

In all likelihood, you're already using iCloud and signed in or signed up when we set up your Mac in Chapter Two. If you're not, you can sign in at System Preferences > iCloud, using your Apple ID. From this menu you can also choose which apps you'd like to play nicely with iCloud.

Above: iCloud allows you to access your data across all your different devices.

iCloud Storage Options

Anyone with an Apple ID gets 5 GB of free iCloud storage with their device, which can be enough for some users. Look at it this way, iCloud doesn't physically store your music, movie and app purchases or photos, it just remembers which ones you've bought and allows you to access them elsewhere.

The main reason you'll need more storage is if a large proportion of your storage is taken up by backing up entire iOS devices like iPads and iPhones.

Storage options:

Extra **10 GB** storage   = £14/$20/year

Extra **20 GB** of storage = £28/$40/year

Extra **50 GB** of storage = £70/$100/year

To purchase more storage enter System Preferences > iCloud > Manage > Buy More Storage. This will be charged to your Apple ID credit card info.

Above: There are three options for how much extra storage to buy.

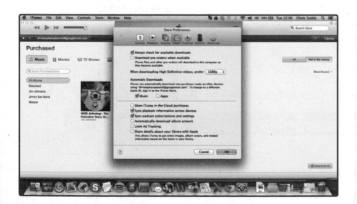

Above: You can have your purchased items automatically downloaded.

Hot Tip

iCloud is useful for syncing data across devices, and if you go to iTunes > Preferences > Store and select Automatic downloads, music and apps your purchases will automatically be downloaded to your Mac.

OTHER CLOUD BACK-UP SERVICES

Aside from iCloud, there are loads of ways to back up your data online and prevent the disaster of lost files and memories. They all offer some degree of free storage and allow you to save and sync documents straight to folders stored on your Mac, making them available everywhere.

Dropbox

Dropbox is one of the current leaders in the marketplace. It offers multi-platform support (Android, iOS, Mac, PC) and offers 2.5 GB of free storage.

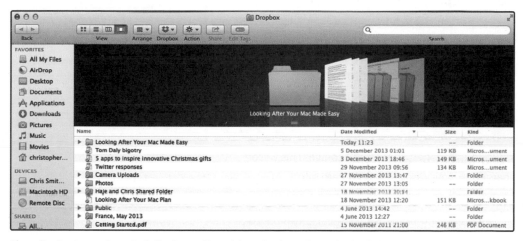

Above: Dropbox is a popular method of backing up files and also makes sharing them with other devices easy.

Google Drive

If you use Google Mail and Google Docs, then Google Drive might be the storage solution for you. It gives you a whopping 15 GB of free storage (spread across your Google Accounts).

SkyDrive

If you're a Microsoft loyalist (Hotmail, Outlook, etc.) and have a PC at home too, you may wish to try SkyDrive. It comes with 7 GB of storage, but some long-time users may be able to get 25 GB through promotions.

KEEPING YOUR MAC SECURE

There's more to protecting your Mac than backing up files. You'll need to be prepared to secure your online privacy, keep tabs on your passwords and keep your children safe online.

IS MALWARE AN ISSUE?

One of the main reasons people choose Macs is their perceived invulnerability to the external security threats that tend to strike down Windows PCs. Generally speaking, you've much less to worry about. There are no known instances of the traditional viruses, but one or two adware/malware threats are slowly creeping in as the popularity of Macs rises. In terms of security threats, you're completely safe, security wise, but Apple has plenty of tools to help you. For extra peace of mind, you may wish to install some security software.

Security Updates

Every now and then you'll get a Software Update notification promising only a Security Update. Ensure you download and install these at the earliest possible opportunity. They'll nullify any threats or vulnerabilities Apple may have discovered.

Above: Gatekeeper checks downloaded apps to guard against viruses.

Apps

As we mentioned, the Mac App Store automatically vets all of the applications, but if you download from the Internet, Apple uses a tool called Gatekeeper to ensure these apps have not been tampered with and are not produced by known developers of malicious software.

It will block these apps from being installed. If infected apps are uncovered, Apple's Sandboxing tool stops them messing with other apps and data.

Hot Tip

In Security and Privacy in System Preferences, you can choose from where you allow apps to be downloaded. We suggest you choose the setting that specifies the Mac App Store and identified developers.

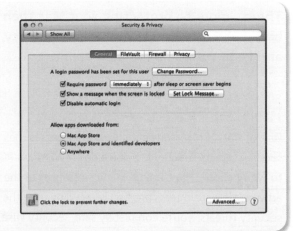

PASSWORDS

Ah, the password. The guardian of everything we hold dear in our digital world. You've probably got loads of them, and if you haven't you probably should have. Here's how they can help you keep your Mac secure.

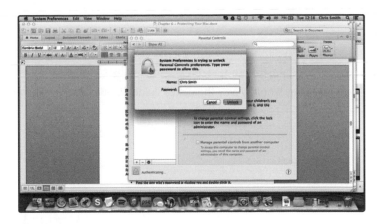

Above: Your system password is required to change computer settings.

System And Administrator Passwords

When we set up the Mac, we created a password. Not only does this let you log in, but is also the administrator password, required when you want to make changes to your computer's settings;

Hot Tip

If you actually feel like physically locking your MacBook as you would a pushbike or a door, then you can pick up some neat solutions online.

for example, by clicking the padlocks in System Preferences windows. You can also make other users administrators.

Remembering Passwords With Keychain

If you're wondering how your Mac remembers all your network, email, Internet and app passwords so you don't have to, it's because of Keychain. If you forget one of your passwords, you can sometimes recover it through Keychain Access in Utilities.

Above: Keychain Access can help you recover forgotten passwords.

1. Open Keychain Access and select Passwords in the sidebar.

2. Find the app the password for which is eluding you and double click it.

3. Hit Show Password and enter your administrator's password (the one you use to log into your Mac) and select Allow. It should now show in the password field.

Locking Your Screen

If you're using a Mac at home or at work, chances are you'll need to leave it unattended from time to time, potentially leaving it open to prying eyes. You can fix this by locking the device after a period of inactivity without having to log out.

1. Go to System Preferences > Security and Privacy.

2. Click the lock and enter your administrator password to make changes.

3. Select Advanced and tick 'Log out after __ minutes of inactivity' and select the amount of time.

4. Alternatively, within Security and Privacy toggle the setting that requires a password to be entered a certain amount of time after the screen saver kicks in.

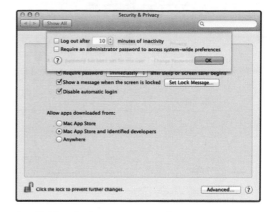

Step 3: Select after how many minutes of inactivity the computer will automatically log out.

Once the screen is locked, it has the same effect as shutting the lid on your Mac or putting it to sleep. You'll need to enter the password to return to work.

Notifications On The Lock Screen

Lock screen notifications, alerting you to emails and incoming messages can be handy, but you don't necessarily want everyone to see them, especially if it's a preview of a sensitive email. You can disable lock screen notifications for each app by heading to System Preferences > Notifications and unticking the 'Show in lock screen' box for each app.

Above: Deselect Show notifications on lock screen.

Logging Out

If you're on a Mac that has multiple users it's advisable to log out of your account at the end of your session. Make sure everything you're working on is saved and hit the Apple logo in the menu bar, then just click Log Out. This will take you to the lock screen and will require a password from the next user to log back in.

ACCOUNTS

Sharing is caring, and we're happy to let other people use our Mac, but that doesn't mean we want all of our files and documents exposed. That's why it's wise to set up a guest account, or accounts for each member of the family.

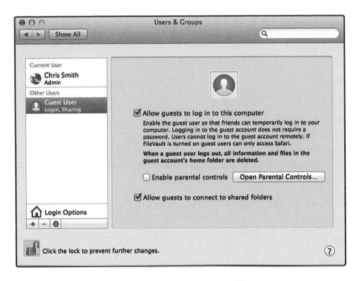

Above: Set up a guest user account specifically for a temporary user.

Guest Accounts

These are handy on the rare occasions someone needs to use your Mac. Head to System Preferences > Users and Groups, hit Login options and tick Allow guests to log into this computer. You'll need to be logged in as an administrator as well. They won't have access to anything you don't wish to share and won't need a password to log in.

New User Account

If other people use your Mac regularly, it's worth giving them their own account. Here they can have access to all apps, their own settings and private document storage. More importantly, they won't be messing with yours. Effectively it creates an entirely new Mac. To set up a new account:

1. Go to Users and Groups in System Preferences.

Hot Tip

It's always worth having a guest account active. If a thief gets hold of your Mac, and logs into the guest account, then the Find My Mac (*see* page 204) portion of iCloud can track the location.

2. Click the lock in the bottom left and enter the administrator's password.

3. Click the + icon to add a new account.

4. In the pop-up window add the name, password and choose the type of account for the user: Administrator (everything that you can do, they can do), Standard (no tinkering with other accounts), Managed with Parental Controls (good to keep the kids on the straight and narrow).

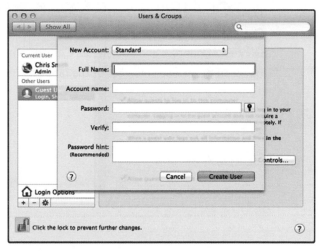

Step 4: Set up the various account details, such as name and password.

5. Click Create, click the thumbnail to choose a profile pic and, if they have one, enter their Apple ID.

Quickly Switching Between Accounts

Anyone with an account can log in on start up, but it's also easy to Quick Switch accounts by hitting the name section of the menu bar, clicking another account and entering the password. None of the current user's apps or data is lost.

Above: To switch accounts, click on the user name on the menu bar, and select another user.

LOST OR STOLEN MACS

We hope this never happens to you, but if you lose your Mac or some light-fingered so-and-so steals it, there's still a chance for redemption with Find My Mac. Otherwise, if you've backed up your data you can reinstall your old Mac on to a new one.

Above: If Find My Mac is ticked, proceed to iCloud.com to track down your stolen computer.

Using Find My Mac

Firstly, go to System Preferences > iCloud and ensure Find My Mac is ticked.

Then head to iCloud.com within your browser and log in using your details. You'll see 'Find My iPhone' but your Mac is also here. If the Mac is in use, you'll see its exact GPS position on a map. Your next step is to call the police and have them help you to recover your property. Vigilantism is not encouraged.

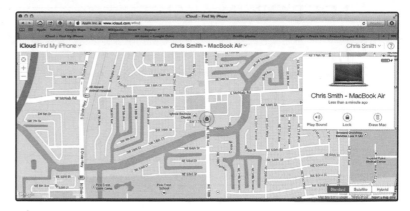

Above: If the stolen Mac is in use, its location can be tracked by GPS and will be displayed on a map.

Locking And Remote Wiping Your Mac

If you think there's no way you're getting your Mac back, you can choose to lock it or even remotely wipe all of the information using Find My Mac. Log in at iCloud.com, enter Find My Mac and identify the device on the map. Click the 'i' icon and select Lock or Erase.

Hot Tip

MacBook Airs are small enough that you can lose them around the house. Within Find My Mac, identify the device, select Play Sound and you should be able to hone in on the alert that sounds.

Above: Through Find My Mac the stolen Mac can be locked or wiped.

MIGRATION ASSISTANT

We discussed this when setting up in Chapter Two. It's a way to move all of your information from an existing Mac or an existing back-up to a new Mac. In this case, as our Mac is lost, stolen or broken, we're moving data from a back-up, so follow these instructions.

1. Firstly, connect the drive to your new Mac either physically or on the same wireless network.

2. Head to Applications > Utilities > Migration Assistant. You'll need to enter your administrator password. This will close down all apps.

3. When Migration Assistant loads, choose the option to move data 'from a Mac, Time Machine backup, or startup disk'.

4. Choose the drive you want to copy from. If it's a Time Capsule you'll need to enter the password.

5. Choose the back-up you want to restore from, and select everything you want to transfer (apps, user accounts and more).

6. Hit Continue to begin the transition. It may take a while, but when you're done you'll have a new Mac exactly how you left it before the old one was lost, stolen or broken.

Step 2: Choose Migration Assistant from the Utilities window.

FILEVAULT, FIREWALL, PRIVACY AND PARENTAL CONTROLS

Your Mac has a huge array of security tools at its disposal beyond the data back-ups and the humble password. Here are some further features the more security and safety conscious among you may wish to deploy.

WHAT IS FILEVAULT AND WHEN DO YOU USE IT?

If having multiple user accounts, iron-clad passwords and a screen that locks the instant you step away isn't quite enough security to give you peace of mind, you should deploy FileVault. It ensures that even if someone does get their hands on your files, then they cannot decrypt that data without a password.

Turning On And Using FileVault

Encrypting your hard drive isn't a step that should be taken lightly. FileVault scrambles everything, only making it viewable to those with login passwords. Should you lose the password and a specially generated recovery key, it's difficult to get access to your data. Only those housing very confidential data should deploy it. If happy to proceed, take the following steps.

1. Navigate to System Preferences > Security and Privacy > FileVault.

2. Turn On FileVault.

3. Add the list of user accounts you wish to be able to log in once encryption is complete.

4. Make a copy of the recovery key and store it somewhere safe.

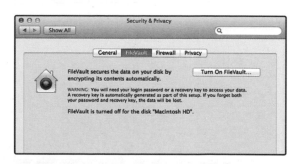

Above: FileVault will give you added security, but it's best to use it only if your data is very sensitive.

5. Alternatively, you can select 'Store the recovery key with Apple' and answer three security questions that can be used to redeem it.

6. When complete, click Continue and then restart your Mac.

Above: Choose which incoming connections to block.

Above: Choose exactly what certain apps have access to.

PUTTING UP A FIREWALL

The Firewall protects you from unwanted incoming Internet traffic. What this means is that nothing can connect to your computer unless you want it to. It's advised that you turn Firewall on in Security and Privacy.

To Block Or Not To Block

By clicking the Firewall Options button, you can modify which incoming connections to select. You can block all incoming connections that aren't for 'basic internet services' and even go into 'stealth mode' that will hide your Mac completely from unwanted communications.

CONFIGURING PRIVACY SETTINGS

The Privacy section of System Preferences deals with the applications you have installed on your computer and what exactly those apps are allowed to access.

Above: Turn off location services to keep your whereabouts hidden.

What Can Access What?

When other applications request permission to access apps like Calendar, Contacts and Reminders that information will appear here. You can revoke these permissions at any time in the Privacy section.

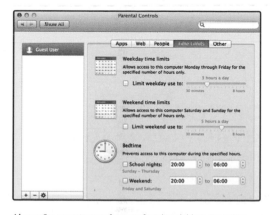

Above: Set up various preferences for what children can access.

Location Services

As we discussed earlier in Chapter Two when setting up your Mac, location services can be great when searching the Internet and using the Maps app, but if you wish to conceal your Mac's location, you can untick location services in System Preferences > Privacy. This will also prevent any other apps accessing your location.

Above: Revoke permission for certain apps to access other apps.

Parental Controls

If you've got kids and they're using your Mac then you may wish to limit the time they're able to use the computer, what they can access online, which apps they're allowed to use, whom they're allowed to contact and more.

Enabling Parental Controls

Firstly, you'll need to create a user account for your young ones (unless you want those controls to apply to you, of course!). Head to Parental Controls in System Preferences and click on that user account (you may need to enter your administrator password to make changes) and then hit Enable parental controls. You can now configure the following settings.

- **Apps**: Add or subtract which applications that user is allowed to access.

- **Web**: Restrict access to the Internet, giving access to only the websites you want them to see.

- **People**: Set up the contacts they are allowed to interact with in apps like Mail and Messages and also configure Game Center activity.

Above: Restrict access to any unsuitable websites.

- **Time Limits**: Set up weekend and weekday time allowances, while setting up a 'bedtime' to ensure they're not up all night.

- **Other**: Here you can restrict assess to the Mac's built-in camera, stop them changing the password and even hide swear words in the dictionary.

- Click the lock again to save these changes.

Above: Other options include hiding profanities in the dictionary.

GENERAL ONLINE SECURITY TIPS

During this chapter we've furnished you with everything you need to know about keeping your Mac secure, but we'd feel better if you also have these next few tips about staying safe online at your disposal.

○ **Remember to log out**: It can be a pain, but when you've finished using email and social-network accounts online (especially on a PC used by others) remember to log out of your accounts.

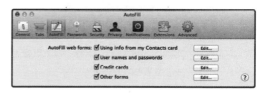

Above: AutoFill can save time but use with care.

○ **AutoFill**: This setting in Safari and other web browsers saves you from filling in web forms by automatically filling things like your name, address, username, password and credit card numbers. It's very useful, but be mindful of who has access to your web browser if you're using it.

○ **Hacked.** If for any reason you feel the security of any of your online accounts has been compromised – this includes your iTunes/iCloud/Apple ID password – then change it immediately. Clues that you might have been hacked can be your friends receiving spam messages or emails or posts to Facebook or Twitter you don't recognize.

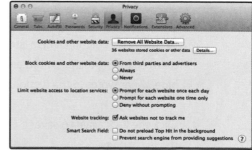

○ **Tracked**: Most browsers now have a Do Not Track request mode, which stops advertisers following you around the Internet. In Safari, this lives in System Preferences > Privacy.

Right: Stop advertisers from tracking you via the Internet.

TROUBLESHOOTING

MY MAC IS RUNNING SLOW

There are many and varied reasons for your Mac having performance issues. If you start seeing that spinning beach ball and programs are slow to react, it may be time to take action.

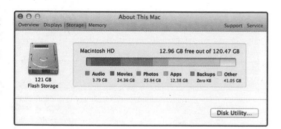

Above: Find out what is taking up space on the hard drive.

FREEING UP HARD-DRIVE SPACE

After a particularly filling Sunday roast, we all slow down a little bit and it's the same with your computer when the hard drive has too much stuff on it. A full hard drive slows performance. Ideally, your hard drive shouldn't be more than 90 per cent full.

Above: The Mac HD Info screen displays available space.

Checking Your Hard-drive Space

The easiest way to see how much space you have available is to select the Macintosh HD icon (click once) and hit Command + I. The information screen will tell you the size of your hard drive and how much you have available. For a more

Above: The bottom of the Finder window will show how much space is free.

in-depth look, hit the Apple logo in the menu bar > About This Mac > Storage. That'll tell you what's taking up the majority of your space. The bottom of the Finder window will also tell you how much you have available.

Moving Before Deleting

Just because you're removing items from your Mac, it doesn't mean you need to delete them. As we explained in the previous chapter, you can move any files you don't want to an external hard drive before deleting them.

How To Delete Stuff

Once you've safely deposited any important files elsewhere, you can set about getting some of that space back. Simply identify the apps, files and folders you want to delete and drag them into Trash. When you're done, you

Above: Right click on files and select Move to Trash to delete.

Above: Deleting items from the Trash is permanent.

Above: When the icons start jiggling, click the X to delete.

Hot Tip

The easiest way to delete apps and games you don't use is to click the Launchpad. Hold down the mouse or trackpad buttons and they'll start jiggling. Hit the 'X' icons to get rid of them.

Hot Tip

If you can't see what's taking up all that space on your hard drive, download a piece of software called DiskInventoryX. It'll index your hard drive and you'll be able to see what's what.

can empty the Trash by right clicking and selecting Empty Trash. Only then will the files be gone from your computer. Warning: once they're gone, they're gone for good.

What To Delete?

Unused apps and games can take up a lot of space and media files like photos, videos and movies can often be a killer. Moving them off your hard drive can save the most space.

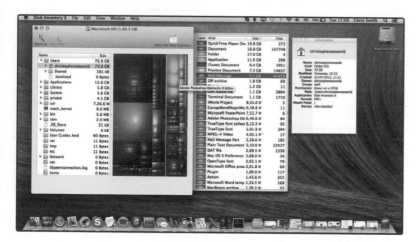

Left: DiskInventoryX is a piece of software which will detail how much space is being used and by what.

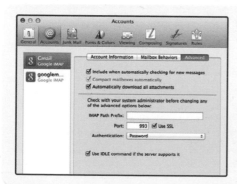

Hot Tip

Wondering why your Mail folder is taking up so much space? Well, it's all those attachments in your inbox. Hit Mail > Preferences > Accounts > Advanced and turn off automatic attachment downloads.

MEMORY

Memory overload is probably the number one cause of slow performance. As we discussed in Chapter One, the RAM in your Mac allows you to keep everything running, but when it gets too much, your computer's efficiency takes a hit.

The Beach Ball And Other Signs Of Memory Overload

If you see the little spinning beach ball pop up on screen when you try to do something, that's your computer's memory trying to summon the power to perform the task. Other signs of memory overload include crashing apps, higher temperatures, a loud fan and the keyboard being slow to react.

How To Check On Your Memory

You can take a look at how well your memory is holding up by opening the Activity Monitor in Utilities and selecting Memory. This will show you a Memory Pressure graphic. The more strain on the memory, the higher the pressure. If the graph shows red, the memory is under duress. In the list above you can also view which apps are taking up the most memory.

Activity Monitor (All Processes)					
Process Name	Memory ▾	Threads	Ports	PID	User
kernel_task	543.6 MB	77	0	0	root
iPhoto	133.9 MB	23	331	5479	christoph
WindowServer	66.3 MB	6	469	4081	_window
Finder	66.2 MB	13	343	1660	christoph
Safari Web Content	64.1 MB	10	241	5564	christoph
com.apple.IconServicesAgent	60.9 MB	4	65	5146	christoph
Mail	57.9 MB	16	415	4386	christoph
Skype	54.9 MB	25	789	4803	christoph
Microsoft Word	53.7 MB	6	207	4175	christoph
Safari	49.8 MB	20	540	4281	christoph
mds_stores	33.5 MB	6	67	114	root
mds	24.5 MB	7	243	62	root
Safari Networking	23.3 MB	4	143	4283	christoph
CVMCompiler	18.2 MB	2	31	5421	christoph
Dock	16.2 MB	7	289	4116	christoph
Messages	16.1 MB	10	242	4839	christoph
Mail Web Content	15.3 MB	11	230	4390	christoph
Activity Monitor	14.5 MB	6	195	5593	christoph
SystemUIServer	14.1 MB	5	297	4118	christoph
systemstats	10.9 MB	2	39	5473	root
diskimages-helper	10.9 MB	3	82	5570	christoph
CalendarAgent	8.8 MB	4	169	4147	christoph

Physical Memory:	4.00 GB	MEMORY PRESSURE	App Memory:	1.25 GB
Memory Used:	3.45 GB		File Cache:	548.2 MB
Virtual Memory:	4.91 GB		Wired Memory:	1.10 GB
Swap Used:	122.0 MB		Compressed:	577.0 MB

Above: If the Memory Pressure graph in the Activity Monitor is red, there is too much strain.

Reducing The Strain

The easiest way to get your computer running at full speed again is simply to quit the apps you're not using. Do this while Activity Monitor is open and you'll see the stress lessen immediately on the pressure monitor. Quitting the apps will also help preserve your battery life. To batch-quit applications hit Command + Option + Escape and Force Quit the apps in the list.

Above: Hold down Command + Option + Escape to access the Force Quit menu and quit any applications causing problems.

High-powered Tasks

Sometimes the strain on the memory isn't due to multiple apps, but one power-hungry application. When editing hi-res photos or editing hi-def video, you need lots of memory, otherwise everything will be done at a snail's pace.

Can I Get More Memory?

In Chapter One we discussed buying and configuring your Mac with sufficient memory. On desktop Macs it's easy to add more, but on newer MacBook models, it's nigh on impossible to do it by yourself and expensive to have someone else do it for you. There are many different requirements for the type of memory you need to purchase and how to install it. Check Apple's support website for details.

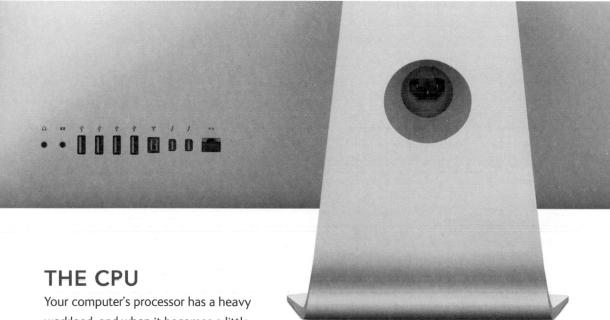

THE CPU

Your computer's processor has a heavy workload, and when it becomes a little too stressed this can also slow down your Mac. Your CPU (Computer Processing Unit) is the something that can't be replaced, but like memory there are simple ways to reduce the load.

How To Gauge CPU Usage

In Activity Monitor, click the CPU tab and you'll see which programs are taking up the highest percentage of the CPU's workload. At the foot of the window you'll also see the Active and Idle percentages. In an ideal world, the Idle percentage should be as high as possible, but if it drops below 50 per cent you could be taking a performance hit.

Above: See how much of the CPU workload programs take up.

Helping Out The CPU

It's quite easy to give your CPU a more comfortable workload by easing up on the amount of apps it has to manage. Quit the ones you're not using, especially the ones demanding lots of power.

> ### Hot Tip
> Is your desktop cluttered with loads of files? Clean it up. It can seriously slow down your computer.

Hard-Drive Failure

A failing hard drive is the most worrying diagnostic for a slow Mac. If you're seeing that spinning beach ball when you try to open apps it could be a sign your storage device is on the blink. We'll talk more about disk maintenance on page 225.

CAN'T STAND THE HEAT

These MacBooks don't half get hot from time to time. They shouldn't, but they do. Sometimes having them on your knee can get uncomfortable and even typing on them can be unpleasant. That's the last thing we want.

Curing A Hot MacBook

As we'll discuss frequently during this chapter, a good old-fashioned reset cures many of the ills you may be experiencing. Give your Mac a power cycle and see if this helps, and turn it off at night rather than putting it to sleep to give it a rest. If that doesn't help, you may need to perform what's known as an SMC reset (*see* page 222).

APP PROBLEMS AND THE GREAT RESET

In this section we'll deal with misbehaving apps and other anomalies within the Mac OS X operating system, and how, more often than not, a simple restart can sort things out.

A RESTART CAN HELP ... MOSTLY

If you're experiencing problems with your Mac a simple restart can eliminate the problem. There are loads of problems a restart can fix, so let's dig in.

Forced Restart

Now and again, your Mac might just decide to restart spontaneously, or will display 'You need to restart your computer because of a ...' message on a grey screen. This is known as a Kernel Panic. There's nothing you can do in these circumstances but bite the bullet. If it happens once, don't worry too much. If it keeps happening, you may have bigger problems on your system.

You need to restart your computer. Hold down the Power button until it turns off, then press the Power button again.

Redémarrez l'ordinateur. Enfoncez le bouton de démarrage jusqu'à l'extinction, puis appuyez dessus une nouvelle fois.

Debe reiniciar el ordenador. Mantenga pulsado el botón de arranque hasta que se apague y luego vuelva a pulsarlo.

Sie müssen den Computer neu starten. Halten Sie den Ein-/Ausschalter gedrückt bis das Gerät ausgeschaltet ist und drücken Sie ihn dann erneut.

コンピュータの再起動が必要です。電源が切れるまでパワーボタンを押し続けてから、もう一度パワーボタンを押します。

Above: If this screen appears, there is no choice but to restart.

Above: The Restart dialogue box will ask you to confirm, or restart automatically if you do not respond within a given amount of time.

Ways To Restart And Shut Down Your Mac

The Mac is teeming with ways to restart. Command + Control + power/eject button cuts straight to the chase; Apple logo > Restart or Control + power/eject brings up the shutdown options. The Mac will start straight back up again. Enter your login password and you should be good to go.

Left: One occasion on which you may wish to perform an SMC reset is if Bluetooth is not working correctly. Follow the steps below to do this.

The Grand SMC Reset

There's a reset and then there's a RESET. Sometimes when your Mac is experiencing problems an SMC (System Management Controller) reset can help. The SMC is responsible for the functionality of the power button, the system fan, which helps regulate temperature, the automatic screen and keyboard backlight brightness, battery performance, charging, sleep mode, trackpad controls and more. Here are some circumstances in which you may wish to perform an SMC reset.

- Poor **Bluetooth** performance.
- **Slow** performance.
- Mac not waking from **sleep** or failing to respond when you open the lid.
- **Power button** not responding.
- **Battery not charging**, taking too long to charge, not showing correct status.
- Fan running **loudly**/Mac running too hot.
- **USB devices** not showing when plugged in.

How To Perform An SMC

1. Shut your Mac down completely (Apple logo > Shut Down...).
2. Connect the power adapter.

3. On the keyboard press the left Shift key, the Option and Command buttons and the power button, all at the same time.

4. Release them at the same time.

5. Press the power button to turn on the computer.

Note: There are different methods for desktop Macs and older MacBooks with removable batteries. Go to http://support.apple.com/kb/ht3964 for details.

The NVRAM Reset

If you're experiencing problems with your computer's audio performance, your Mac starts up from a different disc than the one you selected, or you see a question mark when you start up your Mac, you should perform a NVRAM reset (called PRAM on older Macs). Here's how to do it.

1. Shut your Mac down.

2. Press the power button.

3. Hold Command, Option, P + R before the screen turns grey.

4. Hold the keys down until the computer starts again (you'll hear the sound).

5. Release the keys.

APP WOES

Apps are great, apps are fun, apps turn a Mac into the 'do everything' device we know and love, but they can't half be a pain in the rear end at times. Here's how to remedy the situation when they act up.

Apps Are Always Quitting On Me

Every now and again, you'll notice that all of a sudden an app you're using will crash without warning. You'll get a pop-up informing you that the app quit unexpectedly. Like you didn't know this. Here are a few tips for misbehaving apps.

Frozen Apps

If you're using a Mac with a slower CPU and less RAM, you'll be used to apps freezing on you and that spinning beach ball replacing your cursor. There are two things you can do: wait or quit. It may come around and if you're working on an unsaved item, we'd recommend a little patience. If the app is still unresponsive and doesn't even abide to the regular Command + Q notice to quit, you can Force Quit the app (Command + Alt + Escape).

Tips For Mischief-making Apps

1. Make sure you're running the most recent version of the app. If not, update it online or through the App Store by clicking Software Update.

2. Consider ditching the app completely. Quite often the problem isn't something you can solve; apps have bugs that cause them to crash and freeze. Try an alternative or search the web for known issues.

3. Does the app always crash/freeze when you try to open a particular document? It could be the fault of the file rather than of the app.

4. Perform a system restart; this often irons out wrinkles in apps.

5. Check your disc space and your memory. All of these factors can contribute to app failure.

6. As we mentioned earlier, a hard drive on the blink could be causing problems (*see* page 220).

No updates available.

Good news, you're running the latest version of Skype.

OK

Hot Tip

You can check you're running the most up-to-date version of the software by searching and checking for updates in the menu bar of most apps.

BIGGER PROBLEMS: WHEN A RESTART ISN'T THE SOLUTION

If we've said it once, we've said it a thousand times; a restart solves most of life's (a Mac's) problems, but what about when it doesn't? What about when you can't access apps or open your files without the spinning beach ball popping up? What if your Mac keeps randomly restarting or the display isn't working? It's time to check that hard drive.

USING DISK UTILITY

The first port of call in these situations is the Disk Utility app, which, unsurprisingly, lives in your Utilities folder. We touched upon it briefly when discussing backing up our files. Here we'll be using it for a little first aid.

Permission Decisions

Within the First Aid pane of Disk Utility, you'll see a button called Verify Permissions. Now this is useful as it checks who is allowed to access what on your Mac. When these permissions get in a mess, it can cause apps to act up.

If when you hit Verify Permissions, you're greeted with a list of permissions that differ, you can hit Repair Permissions to patch things up.

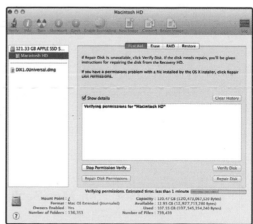

Above: Verify Permissions checks for disk inconsistencies.

Verifying And Repairing The Disk

Think your hard drive may be on the way out? You hear that whirring noise, apps won't open and the fan is blowing a gale? You can check the health of the hard drive by selecting Verify

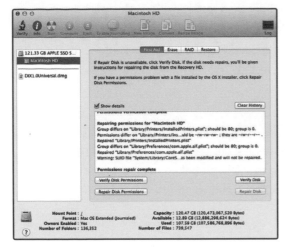

Above: Verify Disk checks the health of the hard drive.

Disk. If all is good, you'll see a green message saying 'The Volume Macintosh HD appears to be ok'.

If the live verification reveals issues, you need to take further steps. You can attempt to Repair the disk.

⊙ **If you have a Mac OS X installation disc:** Insert the disc, restart the computer, hold down the C key and then choose your language and select Disk Utility > Repair Disk.

⊙ **On a Mac with no physical installation disc:** Restart the Mac, press Command + R to bring up the OS X Utilities options and select Disk Utility > Repair Disk. You'll notice there are various options to perform a clean install of Mac OS X and restore your Mac from a Time Machine back-up. We'll get to those shortly.

MY MAC WON'T START

Problems with your Mac can result in the device failing at start-up, leaving you unable to log in and access your files. A blue screen, a grey screen or a flashing question mark usually manifests in this case. Sometimes it won't start up at all. While this could mean a hardware or software failure, there are some steps you can take before calling in the tech heavies.

Steps To Get Your Mac Back On Track

Your first step is to check for the obvious. Is the Mac's battery dead? Is the screen brightness down? Once you've ruled that out, it's time to check the hard drive for problems.

⊙ **Repair Disk:** Follow the instructions above to get to OS X Utilities, select Disk Utility > Verify Disk and, if errors are found > Repair Disk.

- **Try a Safe Boot**: Sometimes performing a Safe Boot then restarting your Mac will bring it back to life. To perform a Safe Boot, start your Mac up while holding down the shift key, and release it once you see the log in window or the desktop. You'll see a host of diagnostics messages, but when this is complete, restart. This may cure the ill.

DISPLAY PROBLEMS

Is your display appearing pixelated? Is it completely freaking out or has it stopped working completely? Don't panic! There are steps you can take to solve this before running to the Geniuses. Before we proceed ... are you sure the brightness is turned up?

Check For Software Updates

Hit the Apple logo and browse to Software Update. If there's an update to your operating system, or a graphics update, install it. This could resolve the issue.

Restarts

The first step in these situations is, naturally, to perform a normal restart. If you don't have any joy there, try the NVRAM and SMC resets outlined earlier in this chapter. There's a good chance this could return your display to health.

Safety First

Performing a Safe Boot can help when Macs refuse to start at all. It can also help when identifying screen issues. Booting in this way allows you to check if the issues persist. If they do, it's likely to be hardware-related.

Still No Joy?

If nothing in this section has solved your problem and the errors are still presenting themselves, it might be time to head to the Apple Store or call support. However, there is something else you can try first ...

A NEW START

You've taken all the steps you can to improve your Mac's performance, updated the apps, maxed out memory, run Disk Utility and repaired any errors, gone through all of the checks and you're still having problems. Sometimes the only way to fix the foundations is to knock the house down and rebuild.

OPTIONS FOR REINSTALLING YOUR MAC

There are several ways to go about wiping the slate clean: you can completely erase your hard drive; you can reinstall the operating system, while keeping all your files; or you can restore from a Time Machine back-up.

Above: A clean reinstall may solve many issues.

Clean Reinstall Of Mac OS X

If there are a few niggling bugs in your system that you just can't shake, maybe a few corruptions here and there, you may wish to try a clean install of Mac OS X.

If you're using a downloaded version of OS X, restart the Mac and press Command + R during the start-up and select Reinstall A Version of Mac OS X from the Mac OS X Utilities menu that pops up. Follow the on-screen instructions.

If you have an install disc or drive then insert it, double click the Install Mac OS X icon and follow the on-screen instructions. Choose your hard drive as the destination for the install and select Options.

From here you'll have two options: to keep the files and settings currently on your Mac, select Archive and Install followed by Preserve Users and Network Settings; if you've already saved everything you need or just don't care, hit Erase and Install. On the next screen you can install the basic version of the OS.

Reinstall From Time Machine

Remember the Time Machine process we went through in Chapter Six? Here's another occasion when it can save the day. Restoring from a Time Machine back-up lets you go back in time to when your computer wasn't so stuttery.

Hot Tip

Once the install is complete head to Software Update to ensure you have all the most up-to-date features (for example OS X 10.9.1 instead of the retail version).

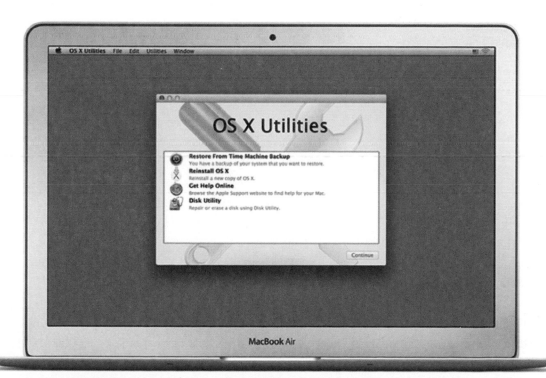

1. Restart your Mac, ensuring the Time Machine back-up drive is connected.

2. Turn the power on and press Command + R.

3. From the Disk Utility menu, select Restore From Time Machine Backup.

4. Select the Drive and the back-up you wish to install from and you're good to go.

There are two points to be aware of here:

1. You should only restore from a Time Machine back-up that was made from that Mac; if you're looking to install the data on another Mac, use Migration Assistant (*see* page 206).

2. Be warned that any data you've saved after that back-up will be erased.

Dealing With Lost And Damaged Files

If you haven't backed up your files regularly and you've accidentally deleted a file or folder, the chances are it's gone for ever. But there are steps you can take to bring it back from the dead. There are several pieces of third-party software you can use to attempt a recovery. See the 100 Top Apps section for advice (*see pages 252–253*).

Revert To Previous Versions

Some Apple-made apps on your Mac automatically save versions of documents you're working on. So if you over-save a document by accident or a file becomes corrupted, you can return to a previous version. In the application select File > Revert To > Browse Old Versions. You'll see a Time Machine-style interface, where you can browse through all older versions and choose one to restore.

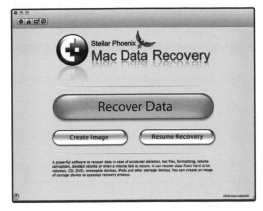

Above: There are various recovery apps which can be used to try to retrieve lost data.

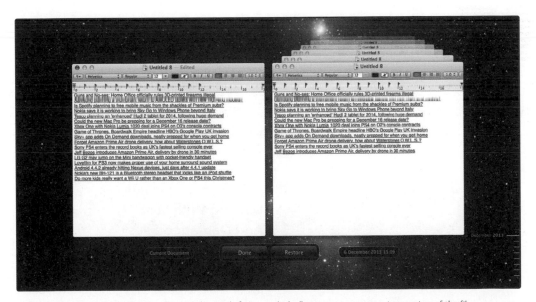

Above: Some apps on your Mac have a Time Machine-style function which allows you to access previous versions of the file.

DEALING WITH POOR BATTERY LIFE

While computing technology continues to accelerate year upon year, we've still not reached that utopia where your MacBook's battery life can last longer than a few hours without the mains.

STAYIN' ALIVE

Before we delve into potential problems with your Mac, the power or the battery itself, let's cover all the basics. There are loads of ways to improve your Mac's battery life expectancy to keep you working on the go. If you take these steps, you should see a dramatic improvement in your battery life.

Above: Various things can take a toll on the battery life of your Mac, for example having too many apps open at one time.

Above: The F5 and F6 keys are used to control the keyboard backlight brightness.

Above: The F1 and F2 keys are used to adjust the brightness of the display.

Adjusting Screen/Keyboard Brightness

The brighter the screen, the more power it consumes. Use the F1 and F2 keys to change the display brightness and the F5 and F6 keys to adjust the keyboard backlight brightness. Every little helps.

Too Many Open Apps

You may not be working within them, but having all of those apps open in your dock takes up power, which takes up battery life. Just like we discussed in the Memory section, keeping only essential apps open helps your Mac's performance no-end.

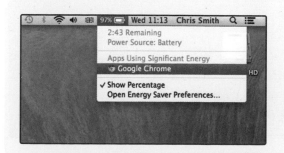

Hot Tip

OS X Mavericks features a neat tool within a drop-down battery meter in the menu bar, which informs you which apps are consuming 'significant battery life'. Shut these down or try alternatives.

Disable Connectivity

If you're not working online, or you're not using Bluetooth, turn them off. Having them constantly search for new networks or devices drinks battery life for fun.

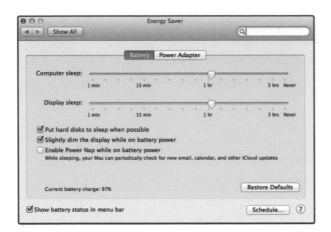

Above: Use Energy Saver to set a certain amount of inactivity time as a prompt to put the display to sleep.

Update To Mavericks

Apple's newest OS makes several behind-the-scenes changes that'll give you an estimated one-hour battery life extension without doing anything. One of them is App Nap. This feature notices when background apps aren't currently performing a task and automatically slows them down. When you use them, they speed up again. To update to the new OS for free go to Software Update and *see* page 52.

Put The Display To Sleep

Within Mac OS X Mavericks, a single tap of the power button puts the display to sleep, thus saving battery life. If you're stepping away for a few minutes you should put the system to sleep completely, by shutting the lid or selecting Sleep from the Apple logo menu. You can also use Energy Saver to configure periods of inactivity when the display or the system will go to sleep.

Above: Turn off the screen saver in order to lessen battery consumption.

Turn Off The Screen Saver

It's lovely to turn your Mac into a virtual photo slideshow when you're not using it, but that doesn't half take its toll on the battery. If you have a screen saver enabled, turn it off in System Preferences > Desktop and Screen Saver > Start After > Never.

Disconnect External Drives And Remote CD/DVDs

You know when you have a disc in your optical drive and you hear that whirring sound of the system checking the disc? That impacts your battery too.

No Battery Back-up(s)

Time Machine is great, but you don't necessarily want your Mac doing that hard work when you're on the train trying to finish some work and your battery life is down to 10 minutes. Within Time Machine, there's an option to disable back-ups while running your Mac on battery power.

Adjust Graphics Performance

On some MacBooks (those with dual graphics cards) you have the option to alter the graphics performance to preserve battery life. In System Preferences > Energy Saver, you'll see the option to optimize graphics for higher performance or longer battery life.

WHAT IF BATTERY-SAVING STEPS DON'T WORK?

The steps outlined above should provide your battery with the ability to run longer without requiring a charge. However, there are still instances where these don't solve the issues of poor battery life. So what else could it possibly be?

Checking The Health Of Your Battery

There's a quick check you can make to ensure your battery is in good health. Head to About This Mac > More Information and then System Report. From there you can browse to Power > Battery Information > Condition. If it says 'Normal' it ain't the hardware at fault; if it says 'Replace Soon' you may want to head to the Apple Store and see about a replacement.

Above: Check whether a new battery is needed in System Report.

Thanks to the aluminium unibody design of most new MacBooks, replacing the battery yourself is not something that is recommended. Don't try. On older MacBooks with a removable battery, you can do it yourself, just by unhooking the catch on the bottom of the device. You'll be able to find the correct replacement by checking the serial number on the existing battery.

Signs The Battery Is On The Way Out

There is only a finite number of charges you can give a MacBook battery before its performance begins trending downwards. Here are a few indicators that it's on the way out.

- **Can't hold a charge at all**: If you remove the power cable and your Mac switches off, you need a new battery.

- **Dramatic drop-offs**: If you're seeing a disproportionate fall in battery life at some stage in the cycle, you may need a new battery.

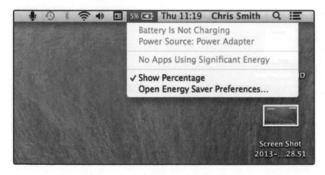

Above: The charger could be at fault if the battery is not charging.

CHARGING ISSUES

If your MacBook battery isn't holding a charge then it's almost certainly down to the battery itself. If it isn't charging at all, then that's a different matter entirely. The charger could be faulty or the charging port could be misfiring. If none of this applies to you or fixes your problem, chances are it is a battery failure.

Faulty Charger

If your MacBook is not charging, the first port of call is to try another charger. The bundled-in MacBook chargers can stand the odd bit of duress, but if you're constantly wrapping them up and taking them on the road, the cables will eventually give out. If a friend has a MacBook, then borrow their charger and give it a try. If that works, you'll need to get yourself a new one.

Software Issue

Sometimes, if a battery isn't charging it could be down to a software issue; your charger is plugged in, the computer recognizes that the charger is plugged in, but the battery is not charging. In these circumstances try the SMC reset explained on page 222. This may solve your problem.

Faulty Charging Port

For years now, Apple has deployed the awesome MagSafe magnetic charging connectors. Before, when you tripped over the charging cable, your Mac would come crashing down to the floor with you, often leading to bent connectors and broken internals. Now the cable just pops right out. However, they're not impervious to damage. They have been known to get quite hot and melt! If that's the case, take it to the Apple Store, warranty or not.

Above: Charger cables may eventually give out.

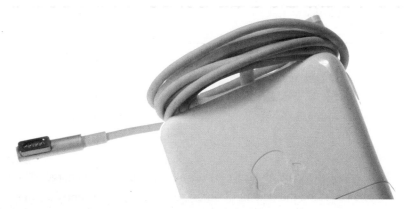

Above: MagSafe chargers are magnetic, meaning that if you trip over the cable, it will pop out safely and avoid damaging your Mac.

KEYBOARD, MOUSE AND TRACKPAD ISSUES

We've come to take the humble keyboard, mouse and trackpad for granted, but if one or all of these bite the dust, your Mac is nigh on useless. Here's how to identify the problems.

IDENTIFYING AND SOLVING KEYBOARD PROBLEMS

There are few things more frustrating than your keyboard deserting you, whether it's USB, Bluetooth or built into your keyboard. Here's how to identify the problems.

Keyboard, Mouse Or Trackpad Not Recognized

If your keyboard isn't functioning at all, it's more than likely to be a connectivity problem. Either the USB attachment is struggling or, in the case of wireless keyboards, Bluetooth is on the blink.

1. For wired keyboards and mice, check the USB connection or try a different port. Failing that, try the PRAM reset outlined on page 223.

2. For Bluetooth keyboards, your first port of call is to ensure the accessory is switched on at the side and the green light is on. Next check Bluetooth is switched on. If all that's in order try repairing the Mac as explained on page 170.

Indicator light   On/off button

3. On rare occasions Bluetooth signal interference can result in intermittent accessory performance. Try to ensure there are no metal objects between your peripheral and your Mac.

Accessory Battery Issues

Bluetooth-powered peripherals have their own batteries, but require very little power. They gain this power wirelessly through the Bluetooth connection. However, you can check the battery level of the device within the respective sections of System Preferences. If it's low, it'll need replacing. Here's some info on how – http://support.apple.com/kb/HT3050

The Keyboard Viewer

To test which keys are being recognized and which are not, you can head to Keyboard in System Preferences and select Show Keyboard & Character Viewer in the menu bar. You'll see it

Above: The Keyboard & Character Viewer will help you identify which keys are being recognized and which are not.

Hot Tip

Before you go running to the Apple Store, there's one time-tested method you can try. Place the MacBook and the keyboard in a zip-lock bag filled with rice. It may just do the trick; the rice sucking out the moisture and returning the keys to working order.

pop up next to the battery monitor. Select it. Now you can hit the keys and it'll show which are being recognized and which are not.

Moisture Problems

Have you spilt anything on your Mac? Have you tried to clean the keyboard with something a little too moist? Come on, be honest now! Unresponsive keys can often be caused by water damage. It's not the end of the world, but it will need fixing.

Using Dictation

If your keyboard isn't playing nicely and you absolutely have to get something down, you can use the Mac's built-in dictation feature. This enables you to speak into the microphone and then translates your speech into text. Head to Dictation & Speech in System Preferences and turn on Dictation.

When within the text field, tap the Function key (fn) twice and start speaking. When you're finished, click Done and the text will appear on the screen.

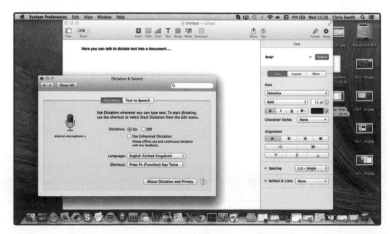

Right: If Dictation is switched on you can speak into the microphone and the Mac will convert it in to words.

I CAN'T GET ONLINE

Such is the modern dependence on the Internet that a lack of connectivity can undermine an entire day's work, ruin plans to enjoy a movie online, or cause social paralysis with the inability to check one's emails. Here are a few troubleshooting measures to help you rejoin the virtual world.

IS IT MY MAC?

Problems connecting to the Internet can be attributed to two things: the connection itself, or your Mac's inability to connect to it. More often than not it'll be the former. Firstly, check if other devices (smartphones, other computers) are able to connect to the network. If so, then it's time to take a look at your Mac's settings.

Above: If your Mac cannot connect to the Internet, check whether other devices have the same problem.

Above: Start the assistant to set up the Internet connection.

Above: Choose the method for connecting to the Internet.

Above: Choose the network you wish to connect to.

Network Preferences

If the signal indicator in the menu bar is full, your Mac has connected to the network but isn't pulling in Internet services. Open System Preferences > Network. If the indicator is green you shouldn't be having problems. If it is amber then hit the Assist Me button and run the Assistant. Quite often, running this resolves the problem. You can also run Network Diagnostics to identify problems.

Software Problems

Occasionally, when a new version of the software is released, it has a few bugs that need ironing out. With OS X Mavericks there was a Wi-Fi bug that interrupted connectivity. Check for known bugs online and keep your eye out for software updates.

Wi-Fi On/Off To The Rescue

If we've said it once, we've said it a thousand times; a restart can do the world of good. Before you restart your Mac

Above: Try turning the Wi-Fi off briefly.

completely, try turning Wi-Fi off in the menu bar, waiting 30 seconds and switching it back on. Quite often this is all it takes to resuscitate the connection.

OUTAGES BEYOND YOUR CONTROL

If your Mac can't connect to the Internet then don't automatically blame your Mac. There could be other factors at play here.

Mo' Modem Mo' Problems

If you're struggling to connect, the first indicator that something might be wrong is the colour of the lights on your modem. If any of the indicators (Internet, Ethernet, Wireless, Power, etc.) change colour from the usual greens and blues to an amber or red (depending on your modem model) the connection isn't live. Immediately restart

the modem following the manufacturer's instructions. If that doesn't work, then it's likely there's a service outage. Call your provider or check for service updates online.

Check The Cable

It's always possible that your Ethernet cable could be faulty. If you're having problems with the wired connection, try to connect to Wi-Fi. If you're successful, it's probably a cable problem. If the same problem persists with a new/different cable, you may need to contact Apple for further support.

Above: If you can still connect to Wi-Fi, the Ethernet cable may be at fault.

EMAIL PROBLEMS

If you're connected to the Internet but not getting your email, or you can't configure your account, there are a few steps you can take to resolve issues with the Mail app.

Can't Configure Account

Apple plays nicely with the likes of Gmail, Yahoo and Hotmail – you know, the household names – but other accounts take a little extra configuration. If asked for account type (POP, IMAP, Exchange, etc.), incoming mail servers and outgoing servers you'll be able to find this information online, depending on your provider. If it's a work account, the easiest thing to do is to call on the IT guys to configure it for you.

Above: Some accounts are simple to set up; others may need more information.

Above: If an email won't send, try quitting the app and restarting.

Email Won't Send

Even when you're connected, Apple Mail has a frustrating habit of refusing to obey your commands to send mail. Sometimes you'll be greeted with a dialogue box that continually demands you enter your password, even though you've entered it correctly. Other times it will inform you the server is unavailable, and others it will sit in the outbox refusing to budge. In all cases you should try quitting the app and restarting, ensuring you save your draft first.

GENERAL MAC MAINTENANCE

Want to keep your Mac looking and acting as it did on the day you removed it from the box? There are a few steps you can take to preserve its prettiness.

CLEANING YOUR MAC

We know it's a bad habit, but when time is short, we often find ourselves eating and drinking while working, and pretty soon our Mac looks like the underside of a sofa cushion. Here are some tips for cleaning.

De-grossing Your Keyboard And Trackpad

Food for thought: the average keyboard contains more bacteria than a toilet seat. If that's not enough to encourage you to keep cleaner keys, then we're not sure what is. For external and internal peripherals, here are some tips.

1. Firstly, turn off your Mac or disconnect the keyboard if it is wired. If it is wireless, disconnect the battery.

2. Use a very slightly damp disinfectant wipe, which you can obtain from your local computing store.

3. Don't use regular kitchen wipes, household cleaners or bleach. They're too wet and could fry your logic board or kill the functionality of the device. Trust us, we speak from personal experience.

4. Using the wipe, lightly rub the trackpad, keys and the dividers until it appears clean.

5. Wipe with a slightly damp, smooth cloth.

6. Dry the keyboard off with a dry, smooth cloth. Don't use tissue or rough cloths or towels.

7. Failure to do this correctly could fry your keyboard leading, in the case of MacBooks, to an expensive repair bill.

Cleaning The Screen

Macs aren't touch screen, but that doesn't mean they don't get pawed by children or sneezed on from time to time. If you've splashed out extra coin on a Retina Display MacBook, then you'll want to keep those extra pixels looking pristine.

1. Turn off your Mac or disconnect the display.

2. Use a dry, smooth, lint-free cloth to wipe away the dust.

3. Use a damp, smooth, lint-free cloth to clean the display, avoiding openings.

4. Dry with another dry, smooth cloth.

Above: Follow these steps to keep your Mac screen clean, especially if it's a Retina Display MacBook.

5. You can also purchase screen wipes from pretty much every electronics store in the world. Invest in these and make sure they don't contain alcohol or aren't overly damp.

ImPORTant Cleaning Information

How about those all important charging, USB and Thunderbolt ports? They can get very dusty and that dust can sometimes harm your Mac's ability to connect to them. Under no circumstances should you use damp cloths to attempt to clean these. It'll fry the inside. Lightly wipe with a smooth dry cloth to remove dust.

MORE HELP IS AT HAND

We've done our best to assist with the most common complaints Mac users suffer, but frankly we'd need a whole volume of books to go through them all. There's plenty of additional help online, while you can also call on Apple to fix your issue.

APPLE ONLINE SUPPORT

While we'd love to make ourselves available to answer all of your questions and solve all of your problems, if you're suffering from one of the rarer problems not mentioned here, you can seek help from Apple's online FAQs or the vast community of helpful Apple enthusiasts who could provide the solution to your problems.

Above: Apple provides online support to help answer your questions and solve any problems.

Above: Select your Mac product for specific advice.

Above: Search the forums for help from others with similar issues.

Above: If you can't find the answer, post a message on the forum.

Apple's Support Website

Before you call tech support or book an appointment at your local Apple Store, you can check online for common issues and instructions on how to use your Mac's features. Head to apple.com/support/mac, find your product, find your issue and make use of the information.

Searching The Forums

The Apple community forums are awash with users who are enduring problems with their Macs. Type discussions.apple.com into your web browser and input your problem into the Search Communities box. Chances are someone else has had your issue and it has been solved.

Posting On The Discussion Forums

If you can't find a solution to your problem, then you can post a question of your own. Fellow Mac users are happy to attempt

Hot Tip

Be sure only to act upon advice within your comfort level. We'd advise against doing anything in 'Terminal' if you're not experienced in this area.

answers as helpful responses earn them reputation points. From the Discussions site , browse to your device's specific forum or to the OS X forums and submit your question. You'll need to log in with your Apple ID. Helpfully, you can choose to receive an alert when a user responds to your post.

TIME TO CALL IN THE GENIUSES

If there's a hardware or software issue that's beyond your skillset, you can go straight to Apple.

AppleCare

AppleCare is Apple's extended warranty service. When you buy a Mac it comes with a one-year warranty. After that you need AppleCare to cover you for tech support, software help, hardware failure and accidental damage. You can call on telephone or in-store support. It covers you for up to three years after you buy your Mac. We know it's really tough to stomach finding an extra £100–200 on top of the expensive Mac you've already bought, but you run the risk of paying out a whole lot more if you don't. Can you afford to be without it? If your battery dies? You'll get a replacement. If your charger is faulty? You'll get a replacement. If the hard drive fails? You get the idea.

AppleCare
Protection Plan

Hot Tip

If you buy AppleCare at the time of purchase, you'll be automatically registered with your proof of purchase. If you're buying after the fact, you can register here – http://www.apple.com/uk/support/applecare/.

Telephone Support

When you buy your Mac, you get 90 days of free, unlimited telephone support. If you have the AppleCare extended warranty, you'll get access to extensive technical and how-to support for up to three years. Usually, they'll aim to solve your problem in a phone call.

In-store Support

One of the few pitfalls of owning a Mac is that only Apple and its authorized service providers can/should fix them.

Hot Tip

If you don't have AppleCare? Give them a try anyway. They might let some useful info slip, or just take pity on you. Hey, stranger things have happened!

If you're having a problem with your Mac, you can head into your nearest Apple Store (they're in most big cities now) and seek help, book a repair, or get a replacement. It's best to book an appointment at a Genius Bar (Apple's pretentious name for its in-store experts) online at http://www.apple.com/uk/retail/geniusbar/ or you can go into the store and make an appointment. If you require a repair, your issue warranty status will determine whether you have to pay for it or not.

If Your Mac Needs A Repair

If your Mac needs attention and you take it to the store, you can part with it there and then. Mostly, they'll fix it within a week. You can pick it up or have it delivered. If you call tech support and a repair is arranged, you can take it to an Apple Store or authorized service provider, or you can have a technician visit, provided you have AppleCare.

One-to-one Support

We'd hope that by buying this book, you won't need this, but if it helps to sit down one to one with a Mac expert to help you master the device, you can book a session at your local Apple Store. You can buy this for £79/$99 a year when you buy the Mac. This book is much cheaper.

Hot Tip

Head to http://concierge.apple.com/reservation/gb/en/workshop/ to find out about free Mac workshops at your local Apple Store.

Your Rights

Under UK consumer law, if you can prove that the fault is Apple's fault and not just general wear and tear, you may be entitled to a free repair or replacement, up to six years after purchase if goods 'don't conform with the contract of sale'. Basically, your Mac would have had to ship with the problem. Try your luck, you never know.

100 TOP APPS

Throughout this book we've focused on the built-in Mac apps, but there's a whole world of third-party software out there just waiting to enhance your computing experience. Here's our top 100 available either online or from the Mac App Store.

GAMES

1. Star Wars
2. Angry Birds Space
3. Call Of Duty
4. Borderlands 2
5. Limbo
6. Batman
7. Minecraft
8. The Sims 3
9. World Of Goo

10. Full Deck Solitaire
11. Lego: The Lord
    of the Rings

SOCIAL MEDIA AND COMMUNICATION

1. Skype
2. Twitter
3. TweetDeck
4. Adium

5. Thunderbird
6. Unibox
7. Sparrow
8. MenuTab Pro
9. Courier
10. Self Control
11. Tweetbot

INTERNET

1. Google Chrome
2. Firefox
3. Opera
4. Pocket
5. Ender
6. Wanderlust
7. NetNewsReader
8. Reeder
9. Transmit
10. Google Earth
    For Mac
11. Transmission

BACK-UP AND ONLINE STORAGE

1. Google Drive
2. Dropbox
3. Microsoft SkyDrive
4. Crashplan
5. iClouDrive
6. Evernote
7. Carbon Copy Cloner

SECURITY AND UTILITIES

1. OmniDiskSweeperX
2. Privacy Scan
3. Disk Doctor
4. Memory Clean
5. Duplicate Detective
6. 1Password
7. Unarchiver
8. Bartender
9. F.lux
10. CleanMyMac
11. Caffeine
12. Healthier
13. LaunchBar
14. Magician
15. Camouflage
16. Temperature Gauge
17. Wake Up Time

PRODUCTIVITY

1. Microsoft Office
2. OpenOffice
3. Better Snap
4. iA Writer
5. Alfred
6. Clear
7. Fantastical
8. iBooks Author
9. Skitch
10. Day One
11. Growl
12. QuickSilver
13. Chronicle
14. Quiet
15. BreakTime
16. Jump Cut
17. CheatSheet
18. Lecture Recorder

CREATIVE TOOLS

1. Adobe Photoshop
2. Final Cut Pro
3. Adobe Premiere Elements
4. InDesign
5. Aperture
6. Touch Retouch
7. Logic Pro
8. Picassa

9. Adobe Dreamweaver
10. Sketchbook Express
11. Snapheal

ENTERTAINMENT

1. Spotify
2. Rdio
3. Kindle
4. DJay
5. Plex
6. Sky Go Desktop
7. BBC iPlayer Downloads
8. VLC
9. Handbreak
10. Delicious Library
11. Boom
12. Vox
13. Capo 3
14. DRM1

INDEX